Why Me & Where is My Happiness?

Patrick Aiken

First Edition
© 2011 Patrick Aiken
New Edition
© 2014 Patrick Aiken
10 9 8 7 6 5 4 3 2

This book or parts thereof may not be reproduced in any form, stored in retrieval system or transmitted by any means-electronic, mechanical, photocopy, recording or otherwise-without prior written consent or permission of the publisher, except as provided by the United States of America Copyright Law.

Cover Design by: XCOPY   Decarlos Stewart
Interior Design by: Sanya Dockery

Published by: Aim High Publishing LLC
All rights Reserved

www.aimhighclub.com
whymeaif@gmail.com
Aimhigh313@gmail.com

Printed in the U.S.A.   ISBN: 978-0615531540

Dedicated To My Loving Daughter Monique Aiken

PATRICK AIKEN SENIOR
The Captain

Content

Acknowledgement *vii*

Introduction *ix*

The Beginning of a Life Changing
 Experience *1*

Now Here is How a Good Thing Can
 Go Bad *7*

Now Here is Where the Nightmare Begins *11*

Monique's Traumatic Experience *65*

Get Ready to Find Out Why We Can't Find
   Happiness and How to Find It   *83*

Get Ready for My Traumatic Cayman
   Experience   *99*

I'm Just Getting in My Cayman Experience   *105*

What's Next? This Calls For Strength   *109*

Acknowledgment

I would like to acknowledge the following for their wonderful support in my writing of this book:

God, for his protection and the strength to endure throughout my experience.

My family, especially my children who have brought me much joy. Monique you served as my inspiration; my brother Ethan "Chicken Man", your support means the world to me.

To my wonderful parents, your prayers and spiritual guidance helped me to recognize that the "Why me's?" could become "Why not me?" and make me stronger. To my hilarious brothers and sisters who continue to keep the jovial spirit of our foreparents alive.

To all others who, in one way or another, helped me make the production of this book possible.

I love you all!

Patrick Aiken

Introduction

This reality text presents sequences of life experiences: that of my own, my daughter's, as well as acquaintances of mine. As you read you will have a better understanding of why people ask themselves "Why me?", and "Where is my happiness?" As you progress you will understand that no matter what situations you are facing, God has your back and will always be there for you. This book serves as a guideline in recognizing symptoms and possible solutions in unpleasant situations.

You will learn how to appreciate your circumstances and how important it is to make some changes in your life. A clearer understanding of how it's possible to create unnecessary stress and how to correct it will be brought to the fore. The importance of God in your life will become even more prominent as you face your experiences.

The Beginning of a Life Changing Experience

Why me? This is a question people always ask themselves when things, or situations come up without invitation, or expectation. I have come to realize that things, or situations that we go through, sometimes we can clearly see: "why?", and how a blessing in disguise these two words can be "**Why Me ?**".

Firstly, I know if we had a choice we wouldn't choose to go through situations that would put our patience, determination, strength, or faith to the test. However we need to know who we really are, because people tend to be strangers to themselves.

The reason we find ourselves in different positions or situations, is because we allow

people or the system to find out who we really are before us finding ourselves, and that is the big disadvantage over our prosperity in our lives.

Secondly, we would be surprised to know the power and strength that is within us. We only need 10% of that power and strength to live a normal life. Some of us however, due to the external forces that present themselves leave us with no choice but to apply more than 10%. We must be cognizant of the fact that we always have 90% more to deal with anything that comes our way.

How surprising is that? But it shouldn't be because often times we go through a situation that we felt like we couldn't deal with, but somewhere along the road we found strength when some people just barely made it. **<u>At that point you</u>** should know that it's your reserved power and strength that you are drawing from.

We often depend on people to help us through what we would call "bad days" through encouragement, even before depending on God for his promised help and strength, and you should always remember that he never fails.

We need to be empowered by what's in us; don't forget you have 90% in reserve ready to rescue you out of every situation.

You are self-contained so you have all the tools to deal with the situations we find ourselves in. God makes a very good partner. In fact, he is all we need to fight the odds.

Isn't it wonderful when we gain, achieve or even make it through a bad situation? Yes I know it feels good but every good thing on the flip side could be bad. You should prepare yourself for whatever comes your way: the good, the bad and the ugly. Nothing is wrong with "aiming high", trying to achieve goals, but if for whatever reason you are not getting where you want to go or what you wanted, there is no limit to trying again.

One of the weapons we use against ourselves is "aiming too high", I know this doesn't sound right but these words are from real life experiences. The reasons for these "aiming words" are because for most people, when they put all their effort in a person, situation or a project and after all that effort they weren't successful, they experience great disappointment and discouragement. The point that I'm getting at, is it really does not make sense for someone to pursue a high end career or business when they know that they don't have what it takes, such as the education or the resources for a specific business.

"When you climb life's ladder one step at a time, you will surely get where you want to go."

If your decision is big jumps or alternate routes towards success, not because that worked for other people and brought them success, there is no guarantee that's going to work for you.

The first route to success is to trust God then believe in "You".

Never depend on anyone but yourself. In a relationship, there should be an understanding that apart from loving each other you are responsible for your own success and achievements. If your partner has a problem with that type of deal in a relationship, that should tell you right there and then that you are heading for a possible disappointment.

Life is too precious for us not to live it to its fullness, so it's time to stop living in denial and take a different approach to a successful life. Don't forget that most of the things that happen to us or the things we go through, we allow some of these things to happen because we saw most of them approaching, but tried to ignore what should have been fixed or changed. I have been in situations that could have been avoided or changed and the list is a lengthy one. There's a year in my life where my life could have been changed for the worst, but because God has been so gracious to me that's why I can assure you how much God cares.

"That same year I started a detailing shop."

This type of business attract people who take pride in their vehicle and I saw it as a progressive business. However, while the shop was operating I needed help with the work load, so I got some people that I knew; in fact some were like friends. So as the business progressed it started to attract people that were enhancing the business. Well, at the time it seemed like what I wanted, people that will support the business and wouldn't have a problem spending. I started having problems with the employees as when certain customers would spend generously at the shop, my employees would have problems about whose customers they were.

At that point different thoughts entered my mind as to why they started having problems, but it didn't take me long to figure out what the reason was why these guys were claiming their customers. Now I started having issues with the direction of my business. Even from planning I knew that this type of business can attract a lot of different people with different ways to success.

"So this is the reason I wrote about some of the things and situations that we found ourselves in; we knew about them or saw them coming."

At this point I created more comfort for my customers because it's all about the revenue. Things started to feel the way I had anticipated so I got comfortable with the way things were.

Now Here is How a Good Thing Can go Bad

"Well that was the beginning of my biggest nightmare because although the business seemed right, the customers that associated with it were wrong for me. So sometimes even though things or people feel right, they are not always right for you."

I can remember several conversations with my parents instructing me not to get in trouble, especially getting "locked up"; in fact they visited us as children, in the USA just to make sure that we were doing well. One of the discussions that we had was that I was too old to go to Jail, and the reason for that discussion was because my family and I believed in what's right.

"Even though we believe in doing what's right that didn't stop me from getting into trouble.

"I grew up in a God fearing family where my parents made it a priority to spend time talking to their children about God's love.

"Encouraging us to always think about what we are doing and make sure it's right for us.

"I really believed in those encouraging words, yet they were not enough to prevent these situations."

So I started applying caution when it comes to my business and actually started to reassess and make changes that were necessary because I was trying to do what was right. During this process, my business was taking a big financial blow, but that didn't matter as far as I was concerned, because it was all about what's right.

Many business associates and customers didn't like these changes because it was affecting their financial gain. So for that reason I started having the feeling that I was in danger. Never would I think that people wanted me away from the business that was 100% my very own.

Now Here is How a Good Thing Can go Bad

One day I got in one of my vehicles that I had parked at my shop, leaving with the intention to meet with one of my drivers. On my way I got a phone call from one of my employees and he asked me, "where are you?" After that call, it was just minutes later my life was changed and before I knew it I was in jail.

Now I didn't know that a person could live in denial for days. While I was in jail, my best friend was sleeping, just to see if it was a bad dream because I would not think that I would ever be locked up. So when I wrote the quote "expect the unexpected", it's because before you know it you are in situations that can be stunning. Even though my business seemed like it was the right business to be involved in, there were things and people that I weren't supposed to be associated with.

"Now we have to be careful about success because it could put you in some bad situations because from the business location to jail I had people thinking why I lived the way I was living. As far as I was concerned I was living a very normal life...

"Based on my position in life, the police officers wanted to find out how I got the vehicle that I was driving, so I told them about my business. They assumed that

the reason was drug related. They had put me in jail, believing that's how I came by my business and vehicles. They held me hostage, wanting me to tell them things I didn't know about. At that point I said to myself why me?"

Now Here is Where the Nightmare Begins

"I started seeing my life flashing back from when I was a child and how I knew that if I did bad things or even told a lie, then I would be in trouble with my parents. I had to get back to the fact that I'm grown and found myself in violation with the law even though I tried not to live a life that would put me in the position I was in."

The acceptance of this reality was now coming to the fore. It was time for me to face my misfortune. I looked up to God for answers and at the same time I needed his help in a different way at that point. My prayers were different because it wasn't about thanks or asking for continuous blessing, so I knew that I was going through a life changing experience that felt devastating.

For those who don't have my experience you can read about them in books or listen to another person's experiences, don't do or get close to anything or problems that will put you in the situation that I found myself in. Do you really want to know why? For me it felt like a thousand pounds was placed on my chest. It was hard for me to breathe. I had to ask God for physical strength. That's not my usual prayer but because I got so physically weak and even though I was praying, it was hard for me to function and this whole jail situation was affecting my mental and emotional side of my life as well. I knew that I needed a special kind of help.

I decided that whatever it took I had to talk to my family about the situation, but, they were devastated. My brother that tries to be strong about things, the situation was so stunning that he wasn't much help to my traumatic situation. I gave God thanks for the way in which he tried.

While being there, I realized that only God's grace would really help me out of this situation that I was in, so I continuously asked for a break through because I was looking at spending years behind bars and money and success weren't helping me. They were just making the situation worst. What does a person do when they have worked all their lives to be successful and it becomes their **Nightmare?**

"Now that's what you would call unbelievable."

At that point in my life, I started learning that people, the system, and the law by which we have to live can be unfair. So I began to pray my way through and out of my situation with the help of a few members of my family; may **God** continue to bless them. Well at that point I didn't have much friends anymore because the best way to know if people who you call friends are really friends, is to get yourself in a bad situation; but I hope no one has to go that far. The point is there wasn't even a tenth of who I would call friends were friends.

From my experience I hope people understand that life is full of adversities, but as time went by, through prayer, I gained strength and got myself acquainted with inmates like myself and found out that some of them had no problem with being there, while others like myself were trying to figure a way out even emotionally and mentally. Well because of the person that I am with my leadership skills, I figured that even though I'm in jail, if I could help someone then my way of life wouldn't be in vain. So I started encouraging the inmates to be strong, trust in God and believe him at his words; that he cares. By doing that, I became strong enough to deal with the fact that I was in jail.

> ***"While I continued to pray for a breakthrough with my situation, I got good at encouraging inmates, my family and even the officers. My main encouragement was that everything was just for a matter of time, and with God's help we can go through any storm or fire and come out victorious."***

Meanwhile back and forth from court, riding in what we call a paddy wagon. We were locked down to the point where we couldn't see outside. The only place we inmates were allowed to see was when we got in the court house. The vehicle would drive into the building where the parking was for those particular vehicles.

During all that traumatic experience, God was in the midst. I went into the court house with handcuffs, chains and shackles, seeing my family looking at me and the position that I was in, I saw the tears building and running down their faces.

> ***"For me it felt like a ball got stuck in my throat and I had to call on God to give me strength to face that judge with the look***

on her face, and remember that the only thing that was working for me was prayer."

So I kept asking God to work out my situation and at the same time work on my lawyer or through him. When the court was in its proceedings, God decided that he was ready to give me another blessing and that was a chance to be free again, that was through the way my lawyer presented my case.

Now the judge that I was worried about, when she spoke to me the entire court and I was surprised that the judge had a smile on her face because being in my situation, you don't normally find a judge smiling.

Now that's what we call God's intervention because she wasn't dealing with me according to my charges. Maybe she didn't see me as an every day inmate and she said, "I'm going to give you a chance to prove your case." She granted a bail in my case, they would figure affordable that I could be on the outside where it would be a more appropriate place to prove my innocence. After several visits to court, finally! The look on the faces of my family members present was priceless. They were giving God thanks and praise.

"Oh! Praise God! That was a glorious moment!"

After living a pretty decent life displaying respect to all, by being honest, caring and even as a person who believes in upholding the law. I was never expecting to be in this type of situation but my experience is a perfect example:

"Of life."

Even though I was living a life that I thought was good enough to keep me out of trouble and at the same time be successful. The fact that I had trust in people that I associated with, I was at risk not knowing that some people can be so heartless.

"So be careful with people that you associate with because not everyone is happy to see you survive or be successful.

"You need to trust God and yourself even though sometimes we can't even trust ourselves because of the things that we put ourselves through; and if someone did those things to us then we would see them as being wicked or bad or a danger to our lives."

We must be aware of our surroundings, because when I came out of jail, feeling so good to be free and getting back to my giving thanks mood. Most of the people that I was associating with, never supported me or even asked my family if there's anything positive associated with my situation. When they saw me, some of them were so ashamed of the way in which they dealt with me, that they told me about this one who went or was in jail, not even to say I'm sorry about what you had to go through.

Then I came to the conclusion that the whole detailing business and those associates needed to be separated from my life because of what I went through. I was ridiculed. I almost didn't know how to start being a part of the outside world again and that's because I was living without trust. I had to reassess and basically start my life over in terms of people that I had associated with, even business associates.

"While I was going through these transitional periods, I kept calling on God for help through these different changes, because on a financial note things weren't that great because of what I went through. But by now you should know that it was God that took me out of jail. Getting the finance together was not the biggest issue because God was in the midst of all that I was going through."

Now for me to make some of these changes in my life, these changes require money and most of all, an environmental change. I got to the point where I couldn't trust anyone that was around and also from what happened to me, I stop trusting people in general. I decided to make all the necessary changes to put my life in a better and different environment, but especially through these tough times I kept asking myself **"<u>Why me</u>?"** because I don't think I deserved all the heart ache.

Through God's help I managed to take my family away from the ungrateful environment – I had to call it ungrateful because I did a lot to build a better community and was dealt a bad hand. However, I had my brother with me all the way throughout those tough times, so we were together in our new environment.

"Now remember the saying that who God bless no man curse?"

This is true because we had blessings on our lives', and regardless of what I've been through or going through, the lord was still blessing us abundantly. At that time it was in the third month of a new year after the bad year that I had, I started to feel that it did not matter what I had gone through. There was still hope based on my situation.

Finally my family got back in our comfortable way of living because it didn't take much for us to be happy as long as we had each other and food. We were according to the Jamaican slang "**good to go**" and what made it better the Lord never left us so we were doing well.

At that point in my life it wasn't about success. It was about living a life that would be comfortable enough, safe from people that's deceiving and also the ungrateful system. The route that I took through God, was bringing success and that was my original Business which was trucking. I was also blessed with a construction Business through my house that I saw being built, so I was having a fantastic year and for that I spent a lot of time giving God thanks.

"My second jail experience was on its way"

Now I was very guarded because I knew the enemy would always have a plan to get in my way of a well-planned life that was set for greatness, and because of that I tend not to take anything for granted, not after what I went through. So I was basically living a cautious, but appreciative life. Despite everything that I've been through, we had a blessed Christmas; we felt that was because I was around.

"No matter what you go through, know that God helped you through."

Therefore you should always be in a give thanks mood. It's the same thing for family and friends. We have to always let them know how thankful you are and at the same time show your appreciation.

> *"Life is not always what you want it to be. You can take control of your life, but what you can't control is when you have to deal with another person's unfair laws that we have to live by. Don't forget that when there is a great blessing in life for you, it is quite possible that you are going to go through some bad things, some we can control and some we can't."*

For these reasons we have to entertain God's help, because it has been a year and a half since I came out of jail and the last thing I was thinking about was going back to jail.

Life and its **"uncertainty"**, before you knew it I was in Jail again. Why this time? Just writing about this I had to sigh, just to relieve all the emotion because this book is a 100% reality and when I was going through all those days, some of them were unbearable.

> *"But you should already know who I have to help me out, if you don't know, it's the almighty God."*

Through God it doesn't matter what you go through or how many times you had to deal with these bad situations, we can't forget that he will always be there. If we got delivered from whatever situations we had before, then we will surely be delivered from whatever comes up again, especially when you are living a clean, honest and God fearing life. Since it wasn't my first time being locked up, I had some experience of how to cope.

<u>At that point</u> it was easier for me to tell God about what I'm going through and also ask for his intervention. One of the things I can tell people is that God gave us a certain amount of strength and he will not allow us to go through more than what we can bear and that is the reason why I wasn't worried about the second arrest, I knew that I didn't do anything wrong and for sure God has my back and my life in his hands.

Now it was the morning of my sister's anniversary and my son Kirk-Patrick Jr's mother's birthday. I was on the road in one of my tractor trailers and on my way home. That's when I was stopped by immigration and the first thing they asked me was if I was a citizen of the USA, so I replied, "No, just a lawful permanent resident." They told me to step out of the truck, which I did. Standing there for about 30 minutes, while they were doing their checks, two officers questioned me about my business. The officer that was checking out my information said to me "Well sir, it seems like you are not going anywhere today." So I ask him why and he said "Well sir, you had a problem and you were arrested a year and a half ago right?" So I said, "Yes sir and the case is not tried as yet based upon the circumstances that surrounded the case." I spoke to him with confidence that they were going to let me go.

The officer said to me "Once you're not a citizen of the country and you get arrested, then you are in violation of the law." This meant I was going to be in jail until I spoke to the judge and it would be up to the judge if he wanted to let me go. Now you know that I'm in for another life changing experience. It seemed these two words were becoming a part of my question to God, so I asked again **"Why me?"**.

"Was this how my life was going to be where once I got to the point where I started being successful then I'm going to be torn down by people and the law of the land?"

"Oh boy" May God help me because I need a fresh set of mercy just to cope.

> *"Now there is a twist in my life because I'm saying to myself how this could be? I'm doing what's right and trying on a daily basis to live a clean honest life. I'm always working hard but I'm being plagued by the system.*
>
> *"Now I had to start seeking answers from God because he knows what we go through*

and for whatever reason, they took me approximately three hours away from where I was arrested and on that same day, I had never seen it hail so hard. For those people who don't know what's hail, it is pieces of ice. I have never seen so much since I have been in that country; even the officers were saying that they didn't remember seeing it like that before."

Regardless of what was going down with me I had to give God thanks because that was just a manifestation of his work, and my little situation was nothing for him to deal with. So throughout this whole arrest and transportation to the place that was going to be my home for God knows how long, God gave me peace in the midst of that storm.

"I had placed the entire situation in His hands and only He could work this out again.

Well at that point I had no doubt that I was going to be out, but the question was, when and where? Whether it's the country I was in or the island of my origin - Jamaica. All that was in God's hand."

Well my family is once again on a roller coaster ride emotionally, trying to find a way around my situation, but that was unsuccessful. Now it was time for me to go to court, so as usual being cuffed, chained and shackled on my way to court, I prayed a different prayer. This time my prayer was not to be free but for direction in terms as to which part of the world to live, because based on what was going on with me, it seemed like I didn't have to do bad things to go to jail.

"My prayer was unusual, in fact I couldn't let my family know that I was praying that kind of prayer. Sometimes we are just in the wrong part of the world and I know not a lot of people think about what country or island they live in, but even though they worry about the stress they seem not to have a problem dealing with it. Well you might want to think otherwise."

I'm now in court in front of the judge and he started to tell me why I'm in jail and that he would advise me to get a lawyer to deal with the situation. That was the end of court and I was leaving the court house to go back to jail with another few weeks to reappear. We all know that even though we pray humanity will chip in and if I had a choice I wouldn't be in that situation for nothing.

"Remember I'm praying for direction as to where to live just to eliminate every

possible way that I wouldn't go to jail or stay out of people's way that run these unfair laws. My answer was forth coming because my first appearance wasn't promising in terms of getting out."

Well I spoke to my family and we got a lawyer to represent me in court, but when I thought that I was getting help I was being robbed by my lawyer. For a certain amount of money, he was going to work the situation out, in fact he told me that he wouldn't take any money if he couldn't help so my family and I had retained him.

Even though we had faith in God that he was going to work everything out I knew that **"faith without work was a lost cause"**.

So we were just doing our earthly part, but I guess the Lord already had things the way he wanted it for me. The lawyer that we got did not even show up at my next court appearance and he had already got his money. So after several court appearances I still didn't have a lawyer. He had already signed the court paper that blocked any other lawyer from getting into my file. That was very clear what and where God wanted me so I knew that my prayer was being answered.

I went back to court and my lawyer was a no show as usual. Right there I had to make a decision. I knew this was not up to my family as I was the one dealing with this jail house experience. I kept reflecting on the nights in jail. How I was placed in a cell with people that were real convicts and that they didn't care about their actions because they knew there was no way out for them.

Now I had to deal with the consequences of their actions so I thought about all that I had to face in the detention facility and I decided I was going to tell the judge I wanted to go back to my native land – Jamaica.

Being the provider for my family, things had gotten very difficult for them and I knew that being locked away was providing no sense of relief. Upon stating my request, the judge comments were somewhat alarming when he stated, "Mr. Aiken, I don't think that's a good idea because you have a very good chance of getting out of this situation." He had somehow seen that I did not deserve this unfair treatment.

In his judgment I was not thinking clearly and so he proceeded to discuss with my family the intricacies of my case. He advised them to seek the assistance of the Bar Association and file a complaint against my lawyer and have him removed from my case.

I interrupted the judge before he could make a ruling. My words to him were, "Your honor, with due respect for the court and my family, I can't do this anymore. My family is falling apart. My children are in need of food and other necessities so I ask the court to release me even to my home country so I can fulfill my role as a father and a provider." Now, I fully understood that not being in the United States meant things would be harder for me but during my incarceration I was producing nothing. Anything for me at this time was much better than not being a contributor.

The reaction of the judge opened my eyes to the fact that God was in my decision. The judge gave me his undivided attention and asked, *"Are you sure this is what you want? Do you realize that you have a supportive family that is ready to go the extra mile for you? I see this as very impressive Mr Aiken. What about your kids?"* I simply replied, *"Your honor, from behind bars I am worth nothing to them and my obligations will not be fulfilled."*

He was quite insistent however on the fact that I stood a good chance of staying in the country. I knew however, the days would turn into years while the system tried to sort me out. I made the only sacrifice I knew best to see them again.

There are times we have to put ourselves in a certain position in order to get to where we want to go. I knew I had some explaining to do to my family as they stood there dumb struck with the decision that I had taken. My brother Ethan, who stood with me through thick and thin, I knew, would be the hardest of all to get through to. However, the explanations would have to come later as I was on my way back to jail for processing.

Back in my chains and shackles the big question popped in my head, *"Why Me? When was I going to be happy again?"* and *"How was I going to deal with this roller coaster life of mine?"* This was where I had to tap in on my reserved strength. I knew God had my back but the human side could not deal with all the pressures of life – I was getting weak. The thought of being stripped of my clothes and asked to bend over and squat horrified me. This was the penitentiary's way of checking for contraband that you might have picked up in the 'bull pen'(the holding cell during your transit to court). Now that thought really killed me! I knew it was standard procedure but I could not bear the continued embarrassment. This felt like the enemy had a plan well mapped out for me, and at least once in everyone's life, you will feel that way. Don't feel bad. It only means you are special or as some would say, 'you're chosen'.

Well, I can't tell you I was cooperative during the ordeal of being exposed as those sections of my body that were being tampered with I considered sacred. Those areas were only seen by myself and my significant other. The correctional officer found it offensive that I was not being cooperative and my situation grew even dimmer when he was assigned to be on duty that night for my block.

God help me! I had no choice but to call on the Almighty. I asked him for patience and protection from this officer who now seemed as if he was assigned to test my faith. I was sure that he must have been informed that I was a trustee and that meant I had certain privileges. I soon realized I was safer with the other inmates than with this officer, as he had his mind made up – I was his target for the time(s) I would be in his care.

It is interesting to note that many persons think they are lords over God's heritage when they are in positions of authority. This was guide evident by the actions of my assigned correctional officer. At times, detainees were often allowed to call their families. His first utterances to me however was, "Aiken! No phone call now!" I expressed my contempt only to be told I had duties to re-arrange the storage area.

The storage area had all the necessary tools to clean the sewage. I was directed to this area and briefed on my task. The correctional officer was closing the door with us alone in this secluded area. Something that was against state policies.

I became somewhat flustered as I was not sure what my fate would be. Being the quick thinker I am, I struck up a conversation with him that threw him off guard. He stated he wanted no problems.

Even though throughout my stay I was tested and tried, I would often get a prompt in my spirit that <u>I was not alone</u>.

Now I'm where God wanted me and I can tell you that I'm experiencing real blessings and working my way to real success, and don't have to worry about going to jail because my community saw me as an asset. I am blessed with countless blessings but still don't trust people in general.

> ***"Well with experiences like mine you can understand that things don't necessarily work the way we want them or where we want to be. We are only humans with needs and wants, so it's likely that we are going to lean on our own understanding; but we should always seek God's direction, because sometimes even though we try to do what's good and try to do the things to stay out of trouble, it's a possibility that unpleasant situations could intervene in our lives."***

Remember the fact is that we don't always go through the same situations, but we all work for the same reason, which is success. We just need to shun the very appearance of a down fall and we could start doing that by taking control of our lives. Even though we see things that will take our lives to the next level in terms of achievements, we have to really spend time, research and be careful of who we associate with. When it comes to whatever you are involved in or about to be involved in, remember not to take any chances, if you see where you could end up in a possible problem, even with the unfair system by which we have to try and survive.

> *"Now changes are not easy but that's one challenge that you need to have full control of because if a situation, business or relationship, for whatever reason is not going the way you want it to go, you should be able to reassess and make changes where necessary. There is nothing smart about staying in a bad situation. Sometimes it may feel or sound like you're giving up but we need to know what, how, and who we fight for."*

Life is a puzzle and sometimes we try to put the pieces where they don't belong. We educate ourselves by listening to another person's life experience, and for the most part they will not be honest with us completely with experiences or advice, etc. We watch movies, soaps, or even read books that are most times telling stories. Well, life is too short for painted pictures. To fix most of these misleading concepts we need to apply more Bibles, more prayer for directions. This book is for all colors and races and applies to each and every one where it belongs.

> *"It doesn't matter where we are; we need to have the key to the door that says success."*

For this reason we try to get an education by going through different stages of learning institutions, and that will always be one of the most assuring ways to success. For that let's not ignore education because by gaining education, it makes us a much smarter decision maker.

"Not having a big education doesn't mean that we can't or will not be successful. In fact, there are a lot of people that are successful without having a degree, but ask yourself if you're street smart, relationship smart and most of all business smart."

The gap to real success tends to get wider without education, but we are all smart until we allow a person to take us for a fool or tell you that you are. You should be smart enough to let that person know that they are foolish to call you a fool. We have to admit that we do foolish things but that doesn't make us fools.

"It's time that you stand strong and unmovable for yourselves; consider you're trying at all times to protect yourself from possible disadvantage from someone else's system or situation."

Decision making is important, you should only make them when you and only you can see things clearly. We have to stop or start breaking down dependency because that's why we often hit a brick wall of unsuccessful things, disappointments and most times we tend to be surprised.

"Depend on you and God to decide, nothing is wrong with advice, but it should be up to you to apply them. Take full control of your decisions and remember that manipulation is not an option. We need to stop for at least five minutes everyday, look in the mirror and ask yourself the question, who am I? At no time you should see yourself as a failure even if your job, your exam, business and most of all your relationship fails, all those things failed, not you. At that point don't forget your reserved 90% that is going to pick you up and generate light, strength and power to move on, not people. Always reach for that starter button to pick you up. Well some people live with a dead battery so they always need a jump start, don't forget that's dependency."

Often time's people depend on your failure or your weakness for their uplifting. The bad times you experience, they use that to measure where they are and how they are living their lives. Even though their lives aren't great, yours is just a confirmation that theirs is not that bad. At that point their lives will not excel the way it should, because they feel you are in a worst situation, so they settle.

"It's a good thing to call on God for problem solving experience, that's how you are going to apply patience to your life because you need a lot of that. Remember God may not come when you need him like a person would, but the difference is he's always on time and you can rest assured that he will solve your problems."

We all need to apply Faith to our lives; we all should know the meaning of faith, let's not get it twisted with hope because it's a whole different thing, but they do work together.

This book contains the key to successful directions, so it's not everything you read is going to be easy; don't forget nothing great comes easy.

"Are you ready for the real challenge?"

Try to live a great life, well I guess that wasn't meant for some of us. Regardless we need to try but we have to prepare to sever a lot of things that you have gotten accustom to, remember I wrote about changes.

By now you shouldn't have any problem making changes wherever its necessary. Now it's good when you start taking control of your life with its ups, downs or whatever direction it's trying to take you.

> *"Let's not get used to not getting what you want or where you want to be, you have the power over failure, disappointment and discouragement. Use that power every day just the way you get up and put your clothes on every day. Take control over your life and its directions. Our lives need to make all the sense in the world, and that's an every day thing. It's not easy to say that every day you're living above the rest of unsuccessful people, but you should feel that way every day and if you don't feel that way, then you need some adjustment when it comes to getting ahead."*

Keep yourself in a position to help a person to get where you have gotten. Through this book you should be able to make a difference. When we ask ourselves the question, is this me, you should be able to say to yourself yes it is me, because you're on your way to a greater and successful life. You should refuse to settle for nothing but the best.

> *"Some things are worth waiting for because you refuse to settle for less. Based upon*

experience, less can become a road block to success. One of the biggest fights you should always be ready for is to fight against poverty. We all know that's the door to hurt, disrespect and disadvantage. So close that door in your life and don't give that key to anyone that you care for, get rid of that key of destruction because that's what poverty is.

"No disrespect to a person that's not displaying success, but at this point you should know you need to be in a different lane down the road. Never stop working hard or even over time to break the cycle of poverty. You need to create good options so you will be able to tell a joker to step aside because you have a life to make the best of."

"You should always believe in yourself, there is no mountain that you can't climb" because life is like a mountain and with a little help from God you should be good to go on, living a successful life.

"Your strength is your achievement because every day it's like getting an Award." So gain strength, stay strong and award yourself every day because only you know what you have gone through or how you felt dealing with your situations. For that reason, you need to come to the realization that you are the most important person to you, we all know that the almighty God is in a different category.

"We should be able to set our weekly goal or achievements because this is how you are going to take charge of your life and its situation. You have to be in full control of what happens in your life. There are times when things are going to happen unexpectedly or beyond your control, but you should not let it slide for a long period of time. Don't forget you have the power, determination and strength to turn any situation the way you want them.

Don't ever get use to that saying easier said than done. Why settle for less when you can achieve the best?"

Don't only watch awards on television or listen to it on radio or even school or jobs, but be in the position to collect your own. That will be a proud moment for you.

Now there's nothing impossible with God and all he ask is to call on him. As the writer of **this inspirational book, I strongly believe in the creator of this universe and through him comes true success;**

nothing plated or covered, so there is no other guidance that will give you a solid success but through God.

"Because of this solid success, you should be able to answer your own questions and tell yourself yes it's me, and because there was a blessing awaiting you that's why all of these things came up, trying to stop you from your success. Greatness belongs to you, take control. How powerful we are in our selves to block out disrespect, disadvantages, disappointments and poverty, which is the leading cause of failure. Live above failure, I know you would want to be reminded of how to live above these bad situations."

"Simply do you, think about you and put you first. You should not have a problem to be the man or woman that you want to be. Crave success, entertain positive people and create a positive environment. They will be an encouragement or more of an enhancement to your positive attitude. Remember depend on God and you for directions."

People will try to redirect all of these positive encouragements, but be careful of people who have no plans to work hard for success; because of that they try to stop you or even show you different ways and how easier things can be, **but life is a game that you need to play by the rules to win honestly, do not forget honesty is the best policy, because everything you do in life comes back.**

"I encourage you to do good things because they will be a shelter over your head and a paved path.

"It's very important to know that your life is priceless and that it's the most important thing ever awarded to you and it will always be, don't forget that it's God's gift to man so you should be careful with your life.

"No one or nobody is more important than you are. You are the most important person on earth; that's the type of value that you have to place on your lives. I know that people, situations, jobs, school, business, economy, the system, the environment, and the destruction of all, poverty will try very hard to make you think and believe otherwise, but not one of these things should take control of your precious and priceless life."

"Now would you stand back and allow any of these things to take control of your life? I'm pretty sure that you would say no or never, but if you don't pay attention it is quite possible that they are doing just that. If you spend more time to remember who you really are, you would not allow nothing or anyone to control or even possibly take over your life. Never forget that it's the most important thing you will ever have.

"Now are you ready to let a person know who you are? You should always be, if the response is not acceptable. Remember, there is a good way how to do it without stirring up tension."

I have discovered that people tend to dig their own pit with their mouth and think that they are defending themselves, nothing is wrong with defending yourself, but you need to know how, when and where. Never forget that your tongue is a small and unruly member of the body that is not easily controlled, especially when you are accused. Think before you defend yourself because there is a way to express or defend yourself without making a bad situation worse. Be humble, be tolerant and you will figure out a way how to deal with people that you think came down on you just too hard.

> *"You are now entering into a life changing experience, by applying to beneficial changes. They will be new to you and you thought you couldn't have done them, but just like a baby, it's okay to creep before you walk.*
>
> *"Trust yourself, believe in yourself and entertain God most of all, then failure will have no choice but to stay away.*
>
> *"Are you ready to say why me in a good way? I hope, based upon achievements good attitudes, great communication skills and a brilliant decision the answer should be yes. So let's get ready for a successful life of constructive desires, goals and vision. You can be all that you want to be, never forgetting that you have so much more power, strength and determination to fight back anything that comes against you, including the enemy.*
>
> *"Have no fear because God is always there.*
>
> *"I myself am excited to write this book. These directive words are from a person*

with experiences. In fact they help me through life's journey. I can relate to a lot of your problems. As you read, share these words of encouragement which stimulate your mind, body, and soul. Be excited to take control of your life, trust only you and God to make your decisions."

We all went through training. As toddlers whether from home, school or church, I know we were taught how to be polite and be nice to our elders and our guardians. The most important lesson however was sometimes forgotten and how to react when we're disrespected, disadvantaged or even abused. Hence, we find ourselves in situations we don't quite know how to respond to.

What we have been taught from a minor, we tend to display all of that and most times they work against us, so what do we do? We find ourselves in avenues that we don't quite know how to get out.

I know that in most areas of a person's life there are people that are placed over us, for example; at work, schools, churches, or even business, sometimes it's hard to deal with the way in which you're being dealt with and I can relate to that, but there's a way out.

At that point you need to assess the situation and deal with it accordingly. Because there are times when we make things slide by for too long and for all that time, we had a problem with the way we were dealt with or was spoken to.

So if we don't take control and deal with things, situations or even people in a respectable manner, things will start bottling up inside and on occasion comes out the wrong way. Always place yourself in the position to express yourself if you have to. The concept that we have been living by; needs to change about accepting or dealing with situation because we don't have a choice; we need to stop compromising our desires. If a person refuses to respect you or treat you the way that you know you should be treated, which is good, then I hope that you will be making plans to make some changes. Don't be strangers to yourselves; take control of your life and the way you want to be treated.

> ***"I can understand if you are placed in a situation that sometimes you don't have the control that you wanted or should have. But that shouldn't mean that you're going to at no time settle or become comfortable, because if it's not what you wanted or what you deserved, then you should know that you have a responsibility to start working on whatever is going against what you want.***

"You have the power and strength over all the things and people that try to suppress you. Now if you want to know how to go about dealing with whatever situation that is not uplifting to you, the first thing to do is to call on God. He will always be there to help with whatever situation you face. Next, depend on yourself; you have the power, strength, endurance and determination that just needs a little stimulating."

You have a lot more in you than you display each day and unlimited control over your life. Don't be afraid to display your power and control daily. We all understand that to gain financially, most of us have to have a job. We are comforted with the word job, but the bottom line is that it's work. Most people get it twisted with having a hobby.

"Most times we face some challenges at work because we create them on ourselves because we went to work not to work. Now if you leave your house heading for your job, you should remember that you are going to work, not to get yourself caught up in different situations and most definitely not in other people's affairs.

Whatever you do in life, especially your job, do it to the best of your ability that you can free your mind, knowing that you deserve what is yours."

At that point you will be recognized as industrious and even in line for an increase. If there is an opening for promotion, you will be most likely qualified. Do your jobs first of all, think about how important your job is to you before you start exposing yourself to different distractions. Think about you, focus on what is more important if it's your check or other people's affairs. Well, even I figured that one out for you. Do well, take nothing for granted use God and yourself for defense.

"Now there is a lot of advantages and disadvantages that surrounds your place of earning and I already outlined the advantages. The disadvantages can be at some point devastating, emotionally, mentally and sometimes physically. Now I know that disrespect is most common around the workplace, but there is a good way to deal with all these issues. Let no one crush your pride and dignity, stand up for you, don't forget that you have the strength and intelligence to deal with or

change anything or people who try to take control of who you are.

"You have the control to fix bad situations. Let's not create unpleasant situations on our selves by doing things that we knew from the start that it's a possible problem. For example, if you have thought about entering a business venture, you should have spent time researching what you're getting into. If you got thus far you should have known the up and down sides to the business."

Remember by trusting only you and God for decisions, you should always see clearly, that whatever transpire during the course of that business, it shouldn't affect you to the point where it's unbelievable, because it is business.

"I know that you would want things to go according to plan but you have to accept that when it comes to business you can't build progress or success on trust, so in all aspects you should deal precisely or cautiously. We need to operate on a more professional level and stop taking business lightly.

"We need to pay a lot of attention and look for the changes and operate accordingly. It's not time to back down, but it's the right time to get more aggressive in whatever you decide to pursue. Today's economy should further confirm that we have to work much harder and also be more attentive to whatever is your involvement.

Never lay back and watch things past you by, especially opportunities. Well the saying is that an opportunity comes once, but from personal experience I can't say the same, because I give thanks to God for several opportunities. Don't ever be relaxed or get too comfortable when you see some signs of possible disappointment.

"Whenever we over look things, that's when a bad situation starts to get worse, for example, whatever you are not clear on when it comes to business, or other situations such as relationships and there are things that are questionable."

You should ask all your questions before you proceed. At that point you should not commit without justification to your questions. If asking these questions becomes a problem or is becoming a problem, you may be heading for a disappointment. We have got to stop regretting the things we say and the commitments that we made.

This book is meant to channel your life in a positive direction. We need to live life to its fullness, but we're only comfortable when things are in our control, so for that reason, take full control of the one thing you and God can control, and that should be your life.

Be the best men and women, boys and girls, its more power and recognition when we live smartly, by having good thoughts and a positive direction.

"In order to achieve what you desire you have to put forth your mind and best efforts, because the more you put in a positive situation, it's the more you can achieve. Don't ever limit yourself, be the role model that this world needs to build a successful nation. You can do it or whatever you chose to elevate or venture in."

Shanika, my oldest daughter was puzzled by her class mates attitude.

I remember she came to me and said she had a problem at school, so I said I know that. She asked me how I knew that she was having problems when she didn't say it to anyone and it's not like she got into any type of trouble. I told her that it was clearly written on her report. She was like, "Daddy, I have a bigger problem", now I'm wondering what could be bigger than her school report that wasn't great.

Now she said to me that she couldn't understand why most of her classmates had a problem with her because it's not like she was mean to them. She always tried to keep a smiling face and on several occasions tried to help some students that needed help with their school work. But that didn't stop them from calling her names. Then I said to her, "Think about why they are having a problem with you".

"The reason why I had to make her think about it was because she was old enough to understand how people operated, especially the fact that she was growing up in a country that was very advanced. So advanced that it's changing people's thoughts. Then my daughter said, "I am just wondering if it's because I try to be nice", because she didn't see that happening to the students that were mean and didn't want to do their assignments; they didn't seem to have any problem. But three of my friends and I are going through the same thing so she asked, "Daddy why me?"

I listened to her trying to figure out the problem, and I tell you I was impressed, but didn't let her know. Then I said to her, "These are the things you are going to experience a lot in this world not only in school, but when you start being responsible for yourself and start to gain financially or even among your associates."

Well I was proud to talk to my daughter like an adult because of her growth. I have always instilled in my children the way the world operates because we know that the society is not operating correctly, but things and people she had to be aware of, because I didn't want to comment on how bad it was about the way her classmates were operating.

I gave her some guidelines to follow because in these days when we try to change some things, especially if we had to confront someone, it can make a turn for the worse. So over time and with careful approach you can change things whether the changes are with you or someone else. I know it was because of the way she operated and her attire because I have to stay successful to keep up with her. She believes in appearance and on different occasions she would talk about students looking at her as if they had a problem with her dressing.

That's how some of us grown people operate, so what do we expect. We have a responsibility to act right, live right and teach our children what's right. But because we are grown if a person should try to teach us the way to live and act with guidelines to follow. We would be mad and our response would be "I am not a child!" We sometimes do more childish things than an actual child. Now my daughter's experience is okay to read about. But what about us grown people? We need to stop the fighting against each other's good attitudes and achievements, because if you didn't know, it's embarrassing and bad when caught.

Our intention is not to hurt ourselves or stop ourselves from success. So we shouldn't be trying to stop or try to hinder another person. People tend to tell you how much they are not a child, then we should let them know grown folks things, such as: what goes around comes around. Now think about that, we have to stop being <u>covetous,</u> and really pay attention to our own issues because every time you discover things about a person or other people, there is something about you that needs the same attention that you are putting on someone else. Let's stop being sorry for our mistakes and think about long-term prosperity. Because our off spring need that and just incase you are wondering <u>why you</u> have to go through some things, just think if you have contributed to your misfortune in any way.

I have wondered <u>why me?</u> For years based on situations that I have been through and these two words would come up mostly when unpleasant situations arose. Not everything that happens to us or situations that come up, we have control over, but the ones that we can control, let's approach and deal with them accordingly, in a manner that they don't come back to haunt us. Earlier in the book I had written about how these two words could be a blessing in disguise. There are things that we face in life, even things that are unbearable, and they are for our own good. These things are just preparing us for bigger and better things to come; in other words they are just making us stronger, that we can cope or manage the things that we all work for to gain success and prosperity.

These two words are also used when we are in denial when good things happen, such as awards, gifts, and also achievements. That is based on hard work, good attitude and loyalty. Even though sometimes we work hard and possess all the good things that are required of us, sometimes it doesn't really matter because not everyone appreciates us, but we have a responsibility to carry out our duties.

It is most likely that good things will happen to us when we do well. In all that we do and get involve in give it your best shot. Don't think that you did good and bad came out from what you did, even if that's how it seems. Don't worry your award is awaiting you down the road somewhere.

In my life time I did so many good things and I'm still not getting the thanks and appreciation that I deserve but I continue, because not everyone that you bless blesses you back or even appreciates your blessings. Don't always do things with an expectation for similar or other favors to return, when we do things, we should do them from our hearts. Knowing that in our life time we have contributed to life in a positive way, whether it is for someone or the society.

Only God knows how sometimes we try our endeavor best to do our jobs or even our relationships, we try to make it work and we are not appreciated. I know from personal experience. It is very discouraging and most times that quitting feeling just starts hovering over us. Then we start feeling like we have come to the end of the road and we are just ready to let go. I'm telling you that when it's time to let go or quit, it should be on your time, because we should have alternate plans and not just quit because someone pushes us.

This book may not be one of the most interesting books you have ever read, but one of the most truthful, realistic and practical books, that will make a difference in every one's life, and hopefully the society that we live in. When I think about the word life, I wonder what's the real meaning because we all know that the breath that we breathe, that's what is called life, but what do we call the ups, downs, obstacles, discouragements, disappointments, misfortunes, our laughter or our tears? They are a part of life and we have no choice but to accept them. Sometimes the only one that we could question is God and sometimes ourselves, because we are able to answer some of our questions.

Mom & dad caring for their grandkids in the USA.

Mom and dad living it up in Florida.

In the Cayman Islands at age twenty.

At our house in MT Vernon, New York, USA my brother Ethan and Natalie on Christmas morning going crazy about crab legs.

Our family reunion in NJ, USA. At this reunion we had a blast. My brother Ethan and his family, Karlette and Marie my sisters, and their family.

My brother Ethan and my sisters Karlette and Marie at the family reunion in NJ.

Cooking up a storm at the reunion; my brother Ethan and I.

My cousin Gary taking in our crazy vibes at the reunion as always.

The boys at MT Vernon, NY my brother Ethan, my dad Vergil and my brother in law Loydie and Gary.

My brother Ethan praying over our back yard cooking, he is the prayer warrier in the family

Monique and I at the Hilton Hotel in Florida.

Monique in the Cayman Islands.

Daddy's little princess Monique.

In Jamaica for our grandmother's funeral; my brother Ethan and I.

My first snow experience.

My father Vergil, his mother and grandkids in Jamaica at our regular family dinner.

Mom and dad enjoying some healthy fast food in the USA.

Our first family business in the USA. Spice Rite Restaurant.

My sister Karlette in her corner doing her thing.

My mom and dad, wonderful woman and man of God.

Monique's Traumatic Experience

"It doesn't matter how successful I got, I had one situation that remained a puzzle for me for many years — the ill-health of my daughter Monique. Diagnosed with sickle cell anemia, she would be admitted to the hospital on numerous occasions. Each time she was admitted I would ask God, "Why me?" Was this another test of faith?

Now my daughter was born with a brutal, deadly disease and I often times heard my daughter from age three years old asking "why me?" She was born a very special girl so she started to walk and talk very early. I don't know if it's because God knew that there was going to be a time in her life that she was not going to be able to walk.

"Monique is the most appreciative child that I have ever seen. She appreciates life and tries to live it with a purpose, and continues to wish that she was a normal child; one doesn't have to feel the pain that she feels. I remember her asking, "Daddy why would such a disease even come in existence"? I'd often reply "Only God knows." This very question had often haunted my thoughts ever since she was diagnosed. Monique said, "Daddy you don't know the pain I feel and I wish other children wouldn't have to go through what I'm going through.

"Monique is my second child and from conception I knew she was going to be a special child. I had a vision that I had to get my life together because this child is going to need all the attention. The fact that she wasn't my first child I was wondering what was the big difference. I just need to

make more or enough money to take care of my family, but that wasn't the case.

The reason for that vision was that I had to be both financially stable and also be ready to spend time dealing with my daughter's brutal disease.

Regardless of what we are going through, the Lord is always there to provide or stay with us and all we have to do is ask him in prayer. Now at this point in my life after my misfortune in the Cayman Islands, I was in Jamaica which is the island of my origin, I would say doing good enough to take care of my family."

Remember the vision that I had earlier, well God had a plan and made a provision for me and my family. Now life is and can be complicated when we don't understand the way how God operates. The first time I went to the Cayman Islands I had a bad experience, but now because God was in the plan, this time around was the perfect opportunity to get it right. When I went there and was on my way back I spoke to a man that was in the government system in the Cayman Islands and was telling him about my bad experience. My remarks were, "If anyone came to Jamaica to me, I would treat them with love and respect."

Now I started to feel like I needed to do more than what I'm doing for a living, even though it was enough. I was at my house when one of my family members came and told me that this man from the Cayman Islands is trying to get in touch with me and it was urgent. Now I had a phone number to call but before I made the call, I knew that it was job related, where, how, and when I didn't know. I called on God just to let him know that I know that this had got to be him.

Well I made the call and even though I knew it was job related, I didn't know God was going to give me what I wanted to do in life, and that was my perfect opportunity to be even more successful. Even though I went through my bad experience, all that was wiped out at that time because God was ready to bless me more abundantly. So when I called the gentleman he replied, "Sir you have been on my mind for a while", I wanted to ask him for how long, which I eventually did, and his reply was about three months ago. That was the same time my daughter was conceived. I didn't bother to get down in the whole vision, so I asked him what was the urgency of the call and I was told in details what I wanted to hear because God was in the midst and that was what he wanted for me.

I accepted the proposal and took my family to the Cayman Islands.

Monique's Traumatic Experience

This time around it was a total different situation where I felt blessed being there. During my time on the Cayman Islands enjoying what I was doing to gain my finance, it was time for Monique to be born, but the date came and there was no sign showing she was ready to come into this world. Now her mother and I were very concerned but as usual I called on God about the situation. We came to the realization that our daughter was being protected by the Almighty because the doctor that was supposed to deliver her, for whatever reason had a few accidents delivering babies that week.

The delays gave us time to find another doctor. However, there were however complications during her birth. The Lord was in the midst of it all though, He prepared us as parents to be accepting of His will towards us even when we found it hard. Monique was the happiest baby after birth. She didn't cry much and to every parent – that's a plus. One look at her and she would smile. Talk about an adorable baby – that's Monique. May God continue to bless her.

When she was two years old almost turning three, one day she was really happy and we were wondering if she was going to continue being sweet and cheery. We never saw our daughter's sickness coming but we all know life is so unpredictable. With that said, we saw that her eyes weren't the same color, they were looking rather yellow but she said that she was fine. She was a smart child so she would be able to tell us if she is not well, because she didn't have any problems communicating or when she needed anything, so I knew that she would let us know that she is not feeling well. Being the loving and caring parents that we were we didn't take any chances. So we took her to the doctor and the last thing we were expecting to hear was that our daughter was sick with a deadly disease.

There isn't a word to describe how I personally felt, and the thing that kills me in that doctor's office is that my daughter was still trying to smile. Now being a loving dad and hearing that my daughter was going to have a hard time throughout her life it made me weak, and I had to pretend that I was strong because her mother was breaking down.

I started to wonder how it could be where my daughter never got sick, and also such a happy child and all that was beginning to turn for the worst. I had to call on God in a bathroom asking him why Monique? She really doesn't deserve to start going through the pain that the doctor told us she was going to experience. That was the first time I started my bathroom prayer because there was a lot more doctors to visit on the way.

Now just the fact that we were at the doctor my daughter started to feel that something was really wrong and she started to get scared saying, "I want to go home because this place is making me sick." Our little daughter started to give us strength by just simply saying I want to go home, because she knew she never felt the way she started to feel, and we have never seen her sick. So I felt that we should go home; we left the doctor's office and decided that we were going to take her home. We made an appointment for the next day to take her to the hospital where they could do further checks.

Now at that time we were still hoping that the doctor would be wrong knowing that we were only human, liable to make mistakes. So I was hoping for a wrong diagnosis. On our way home she started vomiting and all three of us started crying, but for me it was more than what was happening at the moment. It was the thought of even thinking that this might be the beginning of a terrible and painful life for my sweet, loving and happy child. As usual I couldn't let her and her mom see that I was crying. I was so hurt and devastated, but I admire the strength of my daughter until this day.

Monique looked at me and her mother and said, "I'm going to be okay just take me home", at almost three years old. Now I know that she felt that if she gets home then that terrible disease would not bother her, but God knew that was her challenge in life. We all go through our different challenges in life and they are all for a reason. There is the exception however, of when people deliberately allow things to happen to themselves.

Monique's challenges were officially starting to take a toll on her life. We had to turn around and take her to the hospital; now she knew that something was really wrong. Now everyone wishes that their child would be smart, but with what was happening to my daughter I wish if she didn't know that she was going to be sick throughout her life. Why? when the doctor was talking, she heard but I guess the doctor wouldn't expect her to understand, but she did.

On our way to the hospital she was crying and asking, "Why we have to go to the hospital?" She told me and her mom that if she gets medicine she would be okay. Picture how hard that was for us to deal with knowing that this situation was more than just some medicine. Now we made it to the hospital and the doctor that was attending to her was a female and she said to Monique, "You are going to be okay". Monique's response was that was not what the first doctor told us.

You see, even though I was making enough in Jamaica, the lord would have it where I had to be in a different position both financially and mentally to deal with what we were going to go through with Monique. Our daughter knew what was happening without us even telling her. Now this doctor looked on us and said that it was confirmed that Monique had the sickle cell anemia, and we really need to be prepared because one, we have a very smart child to deal with that's not going to agree with some of the treatments, and two, it was not going to be easy to see her in pain but just pray about it.

Monique was in the hospital for six days. What a drastic change in our life style sleeping at the hospital, taking turns between showers and jobs, and there were other members in the family to be cared for. Well with the help from God and Monique's strength we started to accept the brutal and terrible disease that was going to plague our daughter.

Before I headed for the bathroom asking God the question, "<u>why Monique</u>?"because even though I knew that God would allow this to happen for whatever reason, it was easy to accept. Well he gave me peace while I was talking to him and there was a voice saying, "I will be with you always, and that Monique is covered". When I came out of the bathroom the nurse said, "This little girl is very brave and courageous and she's going to be a very special girl regardless of her condition." Well those words that the nurse gave us about Monique being special just gave me a little more strength than what I had earlier. Remember I wrote about reserved strength? I guess it was time for me to reach for mine.

Well it was time for her to go home and we had to set an appointment to go where the head of the sickle cell unit was. Now when we did all that and we were on our way out my daughter looked at the nurses and told them thanks for taking care of her. I was saying to myself how fortunate some children are and not even food they'll say thanks for. Now after my daughter said thanks she had plans for me. She said to me, "Daddy you know we are going to McDonald's right?" I said to her, "Sure if that what you want", because we were so happy just to have her in the vehicle with us again, but she said, "Daddy if you are busy or have to go to work then we could go another time." Let's face it my daughter is a gem to us, she's unbelievable.

Regardless of Monique's situation God was still showing us favor, because if you don't know that she had that terrible disease you wouldn't be able to tell even when she was in a crisis. God would have it that Monique would encourage us to deal with her situation.

She would be in pain and while she is crying, she is still saying that she is going to be okay. Now by this time we went to Jamaica and they ran us through the ups and downs about the disease and that she would have to go to a clinic every month for treatment which were injections or if needed, blood transfusion. When I was there I saw children of all ages, even grown people, so just for my own education I started to talk to people that were affected by this terrible disease and they told me what they've been going through for years. It was not even imaginable I had to say to God; through you all things are possible, because regardless I'm still expecting a miracle.

The enemy wanted us to be mad with God so he sent the social worker to us to basically taunt us because that woman was talking to us like she didn't realize that our daughter was sickly and we were basically in a devastated position. So she told us what no parent would never want to hear. That social worker told us that persons being affected by sickle cell don't normally live past twelve years old. I basically rebuked her, letting her know not my daughter because I knew that God had a job for her to do and she would just be getting ready to start that job at age twelve. Now tell me which parent would want to hear that? I would think none.

When you believe in God you allow people to say what they want to say about you and even go as far as telling you that you will not make it or didn't think you would have made it. When you know how the Almighty works then all we have to do is pray and ask him to have his way and forgive all those who have told you that you would not make it because we all know through God all things are possible.

I had no doubt that my God was going to deliver my daughter despite all the trouble and pain. My daughter is now 16 years old. God is truly awesome. Well we went back to the island where we resided and started to live and deal with our daughter's situation even though it's a tough situation, we had no choice but to accept. Its hard to accept things that you hate like my daughter's situation, well as we all know, life goes on. Even though things were as how they were, we were receiving favors from God and also people that are in the position that would uplift our spirit. I gave thanks everyday for my daughter. She had been through surgeries, blood transfusions and two close calls.

Monique's doctor advised us that she needed a special surgery where they would plant a special tube in her system because her vein were shot, so because of that it was impossible for them to tap into the blood stream. Through all those things that my daughter Monique had to be going through, there was one of those operations that she went through that her mother and I would never forget. We took her to a hospital in Florida, USA, where they could give her all the attention that she needed.

This was when the specialist was planting the tube in her chest. Now we were at the hospital and after being in the hospital several times throughout her life, this time was different. She was a bigger girl physically and older in age so we had a lot of questions to answer that was asked by Monique because she knew and understood more about her condition. When it was time for the sedative drug, she said to us, "I wish I would be the last child that would have to go through this but I will be okay", and she told us how much she loves us. Then she said something that really hit home: She said I am really sorry for to be putting my family through all the stress of dealing with my illness.

Well it was not the first time she told us deep things such as: thank for being there for me and I appreciate you, God bless you. When she said that we told her that we appreciated her for being the daughter that she was and we were really thankful because she encouraged us and at all times she would surprise us with her strength. After the sedation we were with her for awhile until it started to take effect, so the nurse came and got her and her mother said to her, "We will be waiting for you." By now the drug had almost reach its full effect. Monique said, "No matter what I will be back", with a slurred speech.

That operation was supposed to last two hours, just imagine how we felt waiting for our daughter as we prayed. We basically needed a boost of strength because we were nervous but as usual we knew God was still on our side. Well two hours came we didn't hear anything.

We were up to two and a half hours, so we enquirered what was going on. The nurse said, "The operation is done but she will be back to let us know if everything is okay. Now based on experience, when things are good they normally come out and say the operation was successful, but we didn't hear that. Now that wasn't comforting so we waited over three and a half hours before the doctor came out and said, "Mr. and Mrs. Aiken I'm afraid—", before the doctor could finish his sentence, I lost my strength and her mother started crying. Then I told the doctor that I know that she's going to be okay. The doctor told us that the operation was successful but Monique was taking a long time to wake-up. He didn't want to say that she had brain damage but that's what happened.

Now how much more can one little girl bear? After the doctor went in and was in there for about an hour, he invited us in and as usual when my daughter is in the hospital every month or two and I am not there, it's like she'll never get better. So I said, "God I believe in you, so when I walk in that operating room go before me and touch my daughter."

When we walked in, the doctor said, "I think she has brain damage and I have seen this before and when she wakes up we will determine how bad it is." I walked over to my daughter and gave her a kiss and told her remember you promised mommy that you will see her soon. I know my daughter was breathing but her body was lifeless and after I spoke to her we saw her started to move her right hand fingers and I kept calling her name until I saw more movements. Thanks be to God my daughter's eyes started to open and her mother and I started to look at each other and said "That's our courageous little girl." At that time it didn't matter what the doctor had said about her brain as long as my daughter had life we were okay. With that, we gave thanks to God for the life of our daughter.

My daughter's eyes were open but she wasn't able to talk. She held on to my fingers even though she was weak as if she was scared to be away again and I felt it. I am closely connected to my daughter so when she cries I cry. I told her that I'll be there for her always and she should not worry and she shook her head That confirmed what I was feeling.

Now she had to be in that hospital for assessment of the brain issue which was a brand new situation. Well it turned out that our daughter, apart from her deadly disease; the operation left her with brain damage after they did their test. After several days they found out that the right side of her brain was damaged and that she will be paralyzed on her left side; remember we took a walking child to the hospital. It turned out that we had to be lifting her even to use the bathroom but we trusted God because he promised to take us through whatever happens. We couldn't afford to not believe him and I knew that he had this entire situation under control because I have seen him work before.

After all this heart wrenching situation with my daughter, days later we met up with some therapist who told us that Monique may not walk for a while but after a few years she will adjust and through therapy she will get better. Now with this new and additional unfortunate situation that my daughter was in, whatever it took to accommodate our daughter we were willing to do so.

Regardless of what impediments that came up in her life, our pledge was to be there. So based up on the severity of her condition, we had to migrate to the USA. Through all of this, God was blessing us in different ways and most of all, was still keeping our daughter alive. Remember I was told by the therapist that Monique wouldn't be able to walk for a long time. Well after a few visits I'm telling you that through grace and mercy my daughter was miraculously transformed where she started walking, and even the doctor and the therapist were surprised at Monique's recovery.

How great is our God? I would say very great because despite her sickness, my daughter Monique has been highly favored by God. My daughter is in her teens and regardless of how she still gets in crisis, the good thing about it, she doesn't visit the hospital as frequent. Monique continues to maintain an "A" average in school. She is blessed with a special education and now she is a pre-med student and her ambition is to become a doctor, and not just any doctor, she wants to work with kids with her condition.

We believe that she doesn't have to say why me because she understands that we all have our challenges to face in life, and that's Monique's. Even though she went through all that pain it was for her and the family's gratification. She is just an inspiration to her big sister Shanika, small sister Abby Gayle and her brothers, and the best part about it is that she loves the Lord.

My daughter's condition and experiences were just a couple of life's heart wrenching situations that some of us have no choice but to face. We can't forget the saying that once there is life, there is hope. Hope and faith in the most high God, is what brought Monique and the rest of her family this far. I know the journey is not over but with perseverance, faith and trust in God I know my daughter's condition will change.

One of the things that has become most common among people is, consciousness, and reality never chips in until things have gotten bad or people start to find themselves in bad situations. Why do we as humans that are born with senses to guide our lives tend to act like we don't know better? Remember, people who know better have tendencies to say to us you should know better and the saying goes on and on. Remember if it's any form of help that you are going to ask, because you allowed these things to happen, the chances of getting help are slimmer.

Situations like Monique's condition, we don't have control over and people understand that, so they will be more lenient with situations like that. While we have good health lets not use our health to do foolishness, because a lot of people in this world would be happy for good health. If you did not know, that's a gift that you need to cherish. Let's not use our good health to mash down our life or someone else's. Don't forget the title of this book. I do hope whenever we ask ourselves the question <u>why me</u>? it's in a positive way.

Get Ready to Find Out Why We Can't Find Happiness and How to Find It

I know life is often filled with frustrations and all of us are plagued with problems at some point; we also wonder where is our happiness. Remember, when we ask the question why me, it's most likely that we are not happy about whatever situation we have found ourselves in. As you continue to read this book you will understand that you are not alone, because most people can relate to what you are going through or the situations that you have created.

In fact, the world that we are living in today, people have gravitated to things that do not create real happiness and that's why we have to be asking these questions. So I'm ready to help create some ways so we can feel better about our lives. First the key to real happiness is through

God, he promises to care for us. So let's not forget to call on him in whatever situations we face.

In all the things we do in life, we always want them to work in our favor and most of all our needs; we yearn for them to be met, because those things will bring us happiness. I assume that at some point we all experience happiness; that's how we know what happiness is all about — through experience.

When we were toddlers there were so many ways that our parents could make us happy and that's by just loving us. They would show it in what we call in these days simple hugs, but that made us very safe and even though depending on our ages we couldn't speak, that didn't stop us from showing that we needed that love and hug.

How happy we were when our parents would give us a toy? I know the answer is very happy. That made us appreciate our parents more, we wouldn't trade our mom or dad for nothing in this world, because we knew where our love and toys were coming from.

So the point is from we were toddlers we knew what happiness was all about and not only that, but knew how to not let go of whatever or whoever made us happy.

I can understand that some of us often try to create avenues or even place ourselves in different positions in our life to make ourselves happy. Do we really know what's ahead of one's life, the things we have to do or the things we can't do and also the sacrifices that we have to make? In fact, we could stop our happiness by the things we do or don't do, and even what we say or shouldn't say.

This book is for different age groups because it's time for reality. We have to start living realistically and stop trying to cheat our way to real happiness, because that's how we can't find happiness and even if it comes, it goes. We have to take things or life one step at a time and it's very important to know the different stages, that's if we recognize these stages, and approach or deal with them wisely. Then we would secure the different stages.

Education is one of the formulas that I personally would encourage anyone to apply if they really need or seek real happiness. To try and achieve some level of education, that will help you to cope with this technological world that we are living in. From my personal experience I don't see how it's going to be easy living a happy life these days without educating yourselves. Why? Not having education, can cause dependency and by now you should know dependency causes disadvantage.

So I would encourage each and everyone just to try and find some time to educate yourselves. Even if you are living a life that you are telling yourself is successful so you don't need education, remember if you have children it is more effective encouraging a person when you have the experience or have your own achievements, whether it's financially or educationally.

Remember that we are trying to find real happiness and being educated you can be a better student, employee, employer, parent, wife, husband or man and woman.

I know that sometimes we have education and we still can't find happiness but I have spoken to a lot of people that have education but are not utilizing it, so I can understand if it doesn't work for them. We are following the different stages of life just to ensure our happiness, so by having education and you are still not happy, then you know that the problem is in another area.

In order to ensure happiness we're going to have to stop putting aside what's important because some things are necessities. I know that the things in life that's good for us we tend to by pass them. Some might not agree but if you disagree you should not be having any problems to deal with the things that's difficult, and the things that call for real hard work, even the ones that are not physical.

Earlier in this book I wrote about things that you need to do to ensure happiness and I will not leave out things that will contribute to your happiness or even things that's stopping you from being happy. So let us grasp all that it takes to make our lives a happy one. I can just imagine how some people try to get it together but in every thing there is a right and wrong way, and there should be a desire to know the right because the wrong things have a way of showing up most times, so most of us are familiar with it.

I often wonder to myself why we meet so many disappointments in life, but I came to the conclusion that in order to be disappointed you must have been hoping, expecting or depending on something or someone, and that tells me that there was effort in trying to achieve or to be in a positive position. For some people the things that they hope for or expect is nothing to bring them happiness, remember it's all about happiness now so whatever you do, hope for or even expect, it should bring you happiness. Even though in these days the positive things are overridden by the negative, we still have to act and think positive.

Not believing in one's self is a destroyer to one's happiness, because that's the beginning of dependence and not being in control of your happiness; you can expect to be sad at any given time. I often remind people how much power and strength lies within them in general, only if we knew the power and strength that lies within us, we would stand up for what we believe. One of the things we need to capture is our share of happiness, because there is nothing that's impossible with God, all we have to do is ask and keep the faith, depend on God, believe him and be patient.

How often do we find ourselves in situations that we would say there is no way I'm going to deal with whatever comes up; that was or is such a burden that you thought that the load was impossible for you to bear but you found strength to carry on and sometimes you don't know how you did it. You shouldn't forget that you have not been forgotten, God is always looking out for us and he is ready to help us bear our burden.

Whenever you start depending on another person to bring or create your happiness, that's when you start exposing yourself to disappointments. There is nothing wrong with being with a person or doing things together, but remember the word "<u>together</u>". That means it's your part and the other person's part, so your part should always be strong enough that if a person withdraws their part, that shouldn't kill yours.

There is nothing confidential when you're involved with a person, whether it's relationship or business. In fact, only God you should put all your trust in and don't have to worry. Remember we have a guide line to follow when it comes to trust for those who read the bible; you should know what it says about trusting a person. For that reason we should just apply enough for the sake of the relationship or friendship. I know it's a tough situation, but we are trying to ensure our happiness. We need to learn how to trust and believe in ourselves because a person would say I'm not going to do this or do that and they still went ahead and did all that they promised that they wouldn't do. Well, that should tell you that if you can't trust yourself how can you trust others?

We have to be firm about our decisions and that's if you're making the right ones. We need to be self sufficient so when you find happiness whether it's from achievements or relationships, we don't have to worry about being disappointed, because whatever we are involved in apart from trying to achieve an education, you should put in enough to make it work. At that point don't leave yourself exposed. Now when it comes to education, you don't have to worry. You can go and get as much as you want because no one can't take it away from you. It doesn't matter how much you allow a person to toy with your emotions and even twist your head up when it comes to business, you simply allow them to do all that because being educated, it should stimulate your wisdom, knowledge and understanding, and with these blessed gifts they should guide you.

We have to have some form of control over what's happening in our lives. Don't misunderstand what I'm saying here, whatever we do we should do it to the best of our abilities, not give all that you've got. We all have our expectations and we have got to put a certain amount of effort in whatever we do or our commitments whether it's a relationship or business, but there is no guarantee in the thing we pursue so we have to prepare ourselves that if things don't go the way we expect them to, we are not <u>stunted</u> and not able to reassess and make necessary changes. Not that we are making room for the negative things, but most of us are so used to negative things crossing our paths that we have to start figuring out ways how to deal with them. The good thing is that if we have faith and confident in God, then we could put those situations in his hands and do our share of work because faith without work is dead, so let's not forget that.

I realize that based upon today's economy, most people have gotten to the point where they're comfortable with just working enough to get by; while there are people who are not able to comfortably deal with their financial situation. We all know that's not how you should be living, because if we are not about to achieve enough whether it's finance or opportunity we will be in a zone that will expose us to embarrassment, disrespect and that's how people tend to take advantage of you.

You may be involved in areas just to gain financially whether it's jobs, investments or business in general, and what you were expecting to gain or achieve from what you put in, is not working out for you.

Your next step shouldn't be a hasty decision because in every thing we do we have to exercise patience and in fact, some times that's all it takes for things to work themselves out. Remember that there is a concern at hand so you know there is a possibility that whatever is not happening, all these things can develop into some unpleasant situations.

Get Ready to Find Out Why...How to Find It

You are working towards happiness and when we fix our problems and correct our mistakes, and we have to go the extra mile just to find out where our problems are generating from. Identify them and deal with them, which I have no doubt that we have the ability to deal with whatever is stopping us from finding happiness. We need to stop seeing things that are beneficial or uplifting to us as a task and even if that is what we are seeing, if it's something to elevate our lives whether they are in a mental, emotional, spiritual and our biggest concern these days financial, we need to figure out a positive way how to deal with them. From experience, you really want to put God first. If you didn't know, now you know that what ever is necessary in life and you bypass it, it is most likely you will have encounter with them again, and for some of us they will come as a surprise or even seem new.

Sometimes we create stress in our lives by trying to live according to what we are told by another person. Your piece of puzzle in life fits only your slot. So when you try to live your life according to how a person wants you to, most times we find ourselves where we shouldn't be, or lost. We could always listen to advice, in fact you could use some advice and apply it to your life, but that is as far as you should go; not trying to live according to someone else's instruction you need to make sure that's what you want.

We are working to maintain happiness so let's admire a role model, but never try to live another person's life.

I realized that's one of the barriers blocking people's happiness, it's because what we see we want, so we don't appreciate what we have or who we have, and as a result of that we make plans to live above our means.

For example we see a person living in a certain environment or in a real big, spacious house or apartment and also the vehicle that they are driving or the amount that they have. Whenever we start getting uncomfortable about not having and also not being able to live the way that they are living at that point, some people will put themselves in a different situation that will definitely stop them from being happy.

We have to live within our means. In fact, when a person works or do whatever they do to gain financially, it should be enough to pay their bills and at least put something out of what you earn aside whether in savings, investment or just have enough for whatever you wish. Don't try to live a life that you can't afford. The fact is that it just causes stress in a lot of ways more than you could imagine. Sometimes it even affects other areas in your life such as relationships, because if we have a financial problem we tend to lose focus and forget what's important. At times we even forget to say I love you or even remind our partner that you still do.

Finance should be the least of our problems, but these days it the biggest of them all. We should realize that financial issues are affecting all aspects of people's lives. Don't forget that it's because God is so gracious to us why some of us are mentally sound.

We will not find happiness or if you think you do, it will not be around for long, if we don't make some changes where they are necessary. It's not impossible to live a comfortable life that will bring you happiness and you could start doing that by stop worrying about what your family, friends, co-worker, business partner, kid, and I hope not wife or husband thinks.

So what if you have to live in a smaller apartment or house or even drive a vehicle that's not costing big money, so the world could see that you are living it up, or even the clothes that you wear may not be the big name brands that everyone tries to get. I promise you that if you start living a life that's comfortable for you and not anyone else, then you will start to experience some real happiness.

I'm not saying that we shouldn't live it up and live big. We all need to be able to cope and be in control of each stage of our lives as they come. For example, if it's school give it your best shot, and if you achieve academically then you know that you are getting in line for success. At that point some of us move on to jobs, business or investments; we need to make sure that we are achieving so that we don't have any problem to handle our responsibilities or deal with what ever positions we are placed in.

Now you just started to gain financially, so I don't see why people would start burying themselves in various debts or financial commitments. The right thing to do is start learning what it feels like to have what you're working for and when you start building a stable life where you have things under control which is some form of savings, then you can decide to reach a higher stage such as housing and transportation.

This book is definitely about helping you in finding your happiness and not to ask why me. This book was written by a person who recognized all his mistakes and putting the corrections in this book, so it's all reality. I know that every one of us wants to be happy and we would be ready anytime to accept anything that would make us happy — well I hope.

I'm here to remind you that happiness starts when you invite God into your lives and because he loves us so much, he gave us special gifts, and one of them is wisdom to have control over our lives. So we have the control over our lives, even when it comes to happiness.

Now for those who are in a relationship or planning

to be in one, relationships can be a beautiful thing, but it's also the most dominant thing when it comes to our lives. Most of us have wisdom, knowledge and understanding, and with these three important things to guide our lives, we still allow relationships to take control.

For some of us, it redirects our lives to the point where our plans are basically out of our control. It's all about happiness so I hope it's safe to start changing concepts that's not working for most of us. Like the saying about relationships it's a fifty, fifty thing but I think it should be a hundred, hundred thing, and that means that people should come together and see if they are compatible.

If you and your partner are compatible then each person should deposit their hundred. The reason why I think we need a hundred, with fifty, I personally don't think that's enough to make a relationship work, because with the amount of commitments in a relationship it needs a lot of whatever it takes to make it work. We all are expecting our relationships to work so we should be ready to find ways and means to make it work.

Not to discourage a relationship but when planning to enter, there should be a readiness or preparation to make some changes and sometimes drastic ones. Never allow <u>emotions</u> to make your decisions even if it's chemistry as some people would say.

Loving a person is a wonderful thing, in fact that's what God wants us to do. You need to identify if it's love or it's just some things you love about that person or want, because we have to make sure of what we are going to be entering in or who we are going to be involved with. When it comes to relationships there are so many things in a person's life that rides on the relationship.

I've often seen happiness toyed with in so much ways and the fact that we are humans, we deserve the best and not what is tossed to us. So we should approach relationships with extreme caution. No matter how you feel about a person, don't just fall, whether it's in love or whatever you do together.

That's why we need the hundred. That will be strong enough to place you or pull you out. If when a person decides to start breaking down the value of the relationship or decides to end it for whatever most time selfish reason, you should be strong enough to deal with the situation. Well for most people that's easier said than done, but when you deposit you should be able to withdraw. For these cautious reasons that's why I think we should deposit our love and devotion and not just give it away because when it comes to trusting a person, it's too risky to be extremely comfortable.

Now we are getting in to some of the things that dominate our happiness and we should be able to attack the barriers and break them down away from our lives, so we can find our happiness and also maintain it. I know that. It's not everyone going to be in agreement with some of the directive words in this book, but for the people that have most of these experiences, I know that you can relate to a lot of what is written in this book. I know that we all would, from a realistic point of view, need to find out our mistakes and also how to correct them, and that's why I wrote about taking control of our lives.

One of the main reasons I wrote about extreme caution when it comes to relationships, is because the relationship that associates with friendship has so much to gain and at the same time there's so much you can lose, so in order to ensure our happiness we have to approach it with God's help. With your hundred that contains wisdom, knowledge, understanding and just enough trust to ensure the comfort in the relationship, but at the same time protecting your hundred from abuse.

You need to know that if a person doesn't care or find out that what they had was just raging emotions and want out of the relationship, then as much as it's not one of the easiest things to accept, you need to know that life goes on. So that's why whenever we decide to enter one we can't give everything, but nothing is wrong with depositing. So at this point you could withdraw and move on.

Don't allow any one to take or control your happiness, because our lives can't be selfishly lived and the reason why is because there are a lot of people who are looking to us to generate or stimulate happiness in them such as parents, kids, wives, husbands and some friends, because it feels so good to be happy and to achieve success, and success brings comfort. We need to illuminate any and everything that would stop us from being comfortable and we all know that when we are comfortable then happiness starts generating. Then we don't have to ask the question why me in a negative way and have to be wondering where is our happiness. Only if we can detect our problems at each and every point they are generating from, will things be better for us, with the understanding that it's our responsibility to get the ball rolling.

Get Ready for My Traumatic Cayman Experience

There is one thing that I have discovered and it's becoming an epidemic and it is that people, or I should say some people, are just simply not genuine. They are not honest in their association with each other or even with the things that they say. I understand we are living in a competitive world but I have experienced people who try to do or say things to redirect people's mind, ideas, plans and even things that's in progress, but the way that they are trying to redirect or stop your endeavor may be surprising but don't be, because this is from experience.

The way they try, they compliment you on whatever you're trying to accomplish. Now if someone encourages or compliments you on whatever, you would figure that they are being nice or they're with whatever you're doing. In a lot of cases they don't mean what they say <u>watch out!</u>

Life is full of surprises so you should expect the unexpected. There are things that we learn about people's desire towards us and they are not pleasant things. Be careful because it gets worse if that situation is not dealt with as soon as possible, whether it's by keeping a distance or approaching them individually just to clarify what you saw or heard, and all of this can be done in a gently manner.

Now if that person flare up about you trying respectably to straighten out that situation, then you know that you should be cautious dealing with that person. It's not worth it getting into a big argument because with some people some things just can't be fixed. There are so many ways that our happiness can be blocked, so there are some things that we have to just let go.

In these days there is no room for mishaps especially regrets because on a spiritual, mental, emotional and physical point of view, we have to be prepared especially these days, where things and people are almost unbelievable with their approach. We are working towards happiness so we shouldn't leave any area in our lives that could possess a possible threat to our happiness and for us to be asking the question, why me? I remember when I was in my teens and got an opportunity to go to the Cayman

Islands in that same year I start feeling I needed to blend in with the boys at my school. Now these boys are the type that does the opposite of what's good so as a result of that they got a lot of recognition by other students, especially the girls. Well, some men, whatever it takes to get the attention of a female we are going that route. Sometimes we are not thinking if its right or wrong, or even the consequences. I was influenced by their ignorance and uncontrollable attitude.

Now it was so close to graduation and that's the time that I should be doing good like I was prior to me feeling like I wanted to blend in. My teacher saw the changes in me that I wasn't the student that he knew, so he didn't waste anytime to deal with what he called a drastic change in me. So when we got our break he said to me, "What's going on?" I told him that all was well. He then said to me, "Mr. Aiken don't play with me, are you trying to take me for a fool? Because you know that I'm not and I also don't play around."

I was wondering what he was talking about because I didn't realize that I was being influenced until he really pointed it out. Let's be careful because sometimes the wrong things don't feel like it's wrong until some one points them out or for some of us, it's just too late. If we start being humble and just listen to constructive counsel, things can change for the better.

I listen to what he had to tell me and his words were, "You have the potential to do well and I wouldn't think that you would want to ask the question why me and why you can't find happiness". His closing words were, "Mr. Aiken don't work towards being a failure, you need to be attracted to positive people, so you might want to change your association" and that was a very brief conversation.

Now that was a little strong for me, but I understood what he was saying because I knew better and the fact that I grew up in a family that's conscious, progressive and God fearing, I wasn't supposed to allow certain types of energy to take control.

Well by this time I'm realizing that I have to be careful of people, even the ones we call our friends. So even though I was excited about my trip to the Cayman Islands, I didn't let any one of my friends know when I was departing. Even though I was asked that question "when are you leaving repeatedly", I simply told each and every one that I would let them know.

Now the mistake that I made was to even tell them in the first place that I got an opportunity to travel abroad. So I had to start developing my wisdom, knowledge, understanding to be able to differentiate when a person is genuine or when they just want to know your business and if possible stop you. If you didn't know, that's very common.

Get Ready for My Traumatic Cayman Experience

Well finally after the arrangements and I would call it a big time preparation because I wanted to give away even my clothes, because where I was going I will get tons of things, in fact all that I wanted. Well by now you should realize that was a total misconception of foreign countries. Well it was time for me to leave my island and head to the Cayman Islands. I got a feeling that was hard for me to describe. I was so happy that there was a constant joy inside, because I was going to another place in the world.

For those who never travelled to a foreign country or have never made plans to may not understand where I'm coming from, we tend to think that foreign is a bed of roses. So my thoughts were good from people to the environment with all big nice houses. I hope I'm not alone on this! When I got to, the Cayman Islands with my wild imagination and an over whelmed feeling, the person that invited me to the island came to get me at the airport. When I saw him, the first thing I said was, "Thank you God for this opportunity!"

Then I told the gentleman how much I appreciate him because I felt that I've met up with one of the good persons that's left on the earth. Well that man did a good job by enhancing my thoughts about foreign by telling me that I was going to be good because the island needed people like me with my talents. Initially I met this gentleman because of my association with the music business, and even though I was young I was the minister of music in my parish back home where I grew up and that made me popular. So with my popularity I was in line for different opportunities and changes.

I'm Just Getting in My Cayman Experience

I was feeling very fortunate and happy at the same time. We rode around for a few minutes as he showed me around; just imagine how I felt. I wasn't thinking not even for a second that we were in the same world with the same people but just a different place and reality was on the way, I was just in a trance.

After stopping several places it was time for us to go wherever I was supposed to be staying, which was his place. Well when we got there he said, "This is it", well I was lost for a moment because I thought he said we were going to where he lived, but we were heading towards a little shed-looking place. So I was lost for a while when he opened the door and I saw a bed and another person. I was moving very hesitant because of disbelief but he insisted and said, "come on in, this is where we are going to stay", so I said, "Okay", not thinking that's where I'm going to be at for the duration of my time in the island.

What would you think when you had all that fantasy of a place that's just luxurious? But I guessed it was time to get back to reality. Then he said to the other occupant which was his female friend, "He will be staying with us for a while." During the introduction she was acting astonished but played it off really good, so I was looking around in the room seeing the only bed and was wondering where I was going to sleep, because there wasn't even a couch for me to sit on or even use as a bed.

I sat on the one chair and realized that dinner was going to be in that same room because the kitchen was in the room. So with all those stunning events my happiness started to fade and I realized that life was not about what you heard, what you were promised or even imagined.

That night my bed was that chair because the little bed was theirs, but while they were snoring I was thinking about my life in my island, where I basically made plans not to even go back there for a while, but what I ran into started to make me realize that sometimes we have things going for us or an environment that was doing good for us, but gave it up because of another person's influence or an empty promise.

I'm Just Getting in My Cayman Experience

"Nothing is wrong with change but a preparation would be good in terms of facts to deal with situations whether good or bad, not like my fantasies about things being good. For the first time I watched every hour go by and pretended as if I was sleeping round about six in the morning when they were about to wake up, but how do you sleep when you have to sit in a plastic chair without even having somewhere to put up your feet? But I made it through the night."

That night felt like it was longer than the twenty four hours in a day, but it was then I really realized the length of time we have in an hour based upon my night not sleeping. So imagine when a person wasted one day, that's a lot of time that you allow to past and we all should know how precious time is.

Now it was time to be up, so not having the privacy, I whispered a prayer to God giving him thanks to see another day regardless of my astonishing situation. Then we said "Good morning", and I was still trying to act right then this guy said to me, "I'm going to let you go with some other guys they will show you a place where you can stand and you'll get some work." He didn't even ask me if I wanted some breakfast.

Now I'm going from happiness to being taken for a fool because I'm used to my breakfast in the morning from I was child and the fact that he didn't even ask me, I started not being a good <u>actor</u> anymore. However, just to not be rude, he introduced me to the guys that I was supposed to go with and looking at the guys not to judge or underestimate anyone, I didn't see anything about them that said 'music', because not even when I'm in the country of my origin the only people that I saw wear the clothes that they were wearing were farmers or construction workers. I kept my composure because my dad, God bless him, always told me not to be too quick to react, take some time and assess the situation.

So we walked for approximately half an hour. Well the good thing came out of that walk was exercise, even though that wasn't my plan, but that was the way to get to the place he told me to go to. When we got there I thought something happened because there were a whole lot of men standing on a corner. Then the guy said to me, "This is it, if you see someone pull up in a vehicle try to get in first, because if you stand around you will not get any work for the day!"

What's Next? This Calls For Strength

Now I realized that I was on my own. I know that a lot of people would wonder why it was taking me so long to get the picture, but this was just the introduction. I recognized that there were other people from my island, so I tried to blend in, but that wasn't happening. I was fully dressed because I mostly took clothes to wear on my music events, in fact thinking more like a music tour.

Then one of the men from my island asked me where in the island I'm from so I told him. Then he started telling me in detail about how to get work from the next day onwards because he told me that no one will pick me up because I was too dressed so they are going to think that I don't know what hard work is all about.

So I was just in training for what was ahead. Now I was wondering how could this be. I left my island where things weren't bad because my parents provided ways how I could survive, so I was basically working with my parents. I gave that up for I would say nothing because I always have a bed and enough money to take care of my little responsibilities. In fact, at that age I was looking to have my own house.

Now I was sad because I was left in a predicament where I would have to fend for myself. Now I am abandoned because the first person who took me there left with a lady that picked him up, and the other guys that were talking to me told me that the pickup truck was coming so he had to go. Then he said, "I will see you, I have a two day job with that man so I will see you."

I was put in a spot that I didn't even know the way how to get back to the place where I was staying. Sometimes we are put in some situations that can be stunning but we have to call on God for help; because of what I was going through, I wouldn't think that all that was possible and remember it was a person that was definitely taking or took away my happiness.

"So I had to call on God to help me in my moments of distress."

I didn't even get the chance to call my family to let them know that I was okay or what was going on. At that point it was about midday and I didn't even eat and didn't know where to go. I didn't really want anyone to know that I was new in town. So I saw an older man about mid-sixties and ask him where I could get food. He told me about a gas station and he gave me the directions, but he wasn't sure because he was kind of new to the island too.

I had no choice but to try and figure out a way to this gas station but as soon as I walked I would say one hundred feet, I saw the guys running in all directions. Now there were cold chills all over me because I didn't see why they were running but I did see two Toyota Hiace buses and a ford Taurus car on the corner. There were some of the guys looking as if they were getting work so I was saying to myself, I can't believe that just as I walked off these people come looking for workers.

My curiousity got the better of me, so, I turned around heading in the direction of those vehicles but then I saw the guys that were talking with the people with those vehicles were being handcuff. I started to freak out because I didn't know who they were. However, I continued to walk towards the vehicles because two of the persons that came with the vehicle were looking at me so running was not on option. One man looking like a giant said, "Sir! Come here!" I went and he asked me where I was going and what I'm doing in the island. I wondered about his authoritative tone, but knowing the person that I am, never afraid of confrontation. I in turn asked, "Who are you guys?" Another person that was with them said, "Just answer the question that the officer ask."

Now I'm realizing that these guys were people of the law. So I told him where I'm from, we don't answer questions until we know who we are talking to. Another individual said, "This is the <u>immigration</u>." I replied, "Okay", not worrying about anything because I knew that I didn't do anything wrong. We spoke and I told them it was my first day on the island and I'm walking just to get myself familiar with the place.

They then asked, "Why are you dressed?" I thought this question was ridiculous, so I asked, "Did I do something wrong? Because I would like to continue my exploring." The guys said, "Don't make us catch you working!"

I said, "Okay sir", and walked off.

Now I'm thinking that this was the plan of the enemy because there was no way a person could be taken away from their normal life and be placed in the situation that I was in and face so much in one day. I figured my way around for the day and through questions got back to where I was staying. I told the people that I was staying with about my day and the man said, "Well you've made it."

I then asked him what about the music business that we spoke of during his visit to Jamaica. He simply replied, "While you are working then we will find some time for music." Then I had to tell him that I had a life well planned out back home in my island and I took up the offer for a better and bigger opportunity.

Well I guess I made him mad because he told me that I had to get a place to stay as from that day. I really don't think anyone wanted to be me. I was basically put on the street. I had to ask how do I get to call home and tell them what was going on, well not everything. But that I was alive because with all that was happening, I had to ask myself what was next.

I had to ask how to get a call to my home island. I needed to inform my family that I was alive and well – of course the negative details could not be shared. I asked the young man when I could call? He said if you have the money for the phone card. You see, we cannot always blame ourselves for something that we go through because when it comes to opportunities, especially our career or desires, because we all strive for better. When there is an opportunity nothing is wrong with taking it, but I always try to tell people to never jump at every opportunity whether it's a job, business or relationship. I know we should be ready to accept opportunities considering the sayings about opportunity, but not everyone is going to work for you. Some of them you may see them clearly and some because you had the experience before, it doesn't necessarily mean it is going to work again. With my experiences in life with a lot of things and people, since I have almost travelled the world, I had to learn the hard way that it's always good to research everything you might be getting into, because that will allow you to make a better decision.

With what I went through I thought it was supposed to be the best thing for me, but it turned out that until today, it's still the worst move in terms of travelling to another person's country or island. That's why it's important for me to share some of my experience because this book is all about real life experiences, some of what I have been through myself and some I have seen.

Being in the Cayman Islands for a week I had to start sleeping in a shed on a construction site. I was talking to a guy that lived at the same place where I was staying, but in a different room. Telling him about my situation, he wasn't in a much better situation except he had a job and he said he had the key to a shed at the construction site that he worked, and that I could stay there because I didn't have the money for a hotel; and in that island, the hotels were expensive and guest houses were always full.

So I had no choice but to take up his offer. Well everything seem to be going bad apart from my little home and because I didn't sleep for a few days, the cement bags wasn't a bad bed, especially the empty ones for the pillow.

What's Next? This Calls For Strength

I couldn't sleep past six in the morning because the workers cames in at six thirty, but not having light the guy who gave me the key to the shed would have to come and wake me up if I fell asleep in the morning, because I have nights that I couldn't sleep. All that changed for the worse when the owner for the house they were building called by phone for the contractor for the site.

Now the owner was standing right at the door and that was about five thirty in the morning. Now his question to the contractor was why the shed didn't have on a lock. I was still inside that ten by twelve shed and there was no where to hide, so he then opened the door and saw me. He was so surprise that he asked me if I was the security and I had no other choice but to say yes. Then his response was that his contractor didn't tell him that he had a security.

I knew I was going to be in a lot of trouble. I had to strategize a way to get out of there before the contractor arrive on the site. So I told him I had to go because I had to work at a different site so he said, "Okay". At that point I didn't hesitate. I started walking and when I got to about two hundred feet he started shouting for me to stop. Now why would I stop after the situation that I was in?

Well I wasn't a champion in running, but when I started that morning <u>and got away</u>, I started to think about a running career because no one could catch me. From that morning I stopped believing in having happiness and my comfort and giving it up for things, place, or people that were full of uncertainty and it further made me know that even if the opportunity looks or sounds good, make preparations that where ever you're expecting to go and expecting all good, on the flip side things could go bad. Being a native of Jamaica and living comfortably, I had the feeling that life could be better being in another country or island. In fact, that was the impression that some people that have travelled gave. Well my experience should clearly tell you that we should appreciate where we are from.

My experience on a whole was very bad, but we learn from our experiences, the good and bad ones and remember some you don't need to have because not everyone gets the chance to tell them. That whole trip to the Cayman Islands was a whole book by itself and in the future we will read more about that experience.

Now I'm back in Jamaica appreciating life, and the comfort of my home.

We should have experiences, but the bad ones that people are going through, we don't have to make them or deal with them. So many of these experiences can cause danger and even loss of lives and the fact that we are working towards being happy, it's not every opportunity or experience we are going to go for. Now the saying is that "experience makes a man".

That's why there are some concepts that needs to be changed in life because most of them were put in place by people that figured the possibilities and heard things. So they put them in place as a guideline and we have been living by them for years. It's time for some reality that's based on real experience.

There are some people that go through things that you can't even share those experiences not even to the closest person to you, but the good thing about all of these situations, is that God knows and he understands all of our situations whether they are good, bad, or unbelievable.

I've realized that people are living without worrying about happiness, but why is that? Is it the fact that we have gotten used to not having or getting what we want? We don't need to defeat the purpose of life, because that's not what God intended for us. I have met up with people that are so contradicting, to the point where they think that there is no happiness for them, but for those who have experienced happiness at some point, already know better than that. It's just to get things right and that's why we have to invite God into our lives.

Let's not pay all the attention to what's going on in the system that's really programmable. It's simply set up for us to go through things where we can be controlled. So if we have things hard, we will not be able to buy things cash, because once we go through the credit system then there is no privacy in our lives. The questions that we have to answer like where do you live, work and even how many relationships you have, don't forget all those references tell's or let's people know your business. We are controlled and those things don't bring happiness, so our intention should be to change some of those locks and get the key to open opportunities. It should be all about our freedom and I truly believe in us that really need a happy life.

For all those that are ready for happy lives, join me in fighting against poverty, manipulation, and to pray for people that fight against our happiness. It is very common among relationships or friends these days that are our companions I guess, tries their best to either stop their happiness or prevent you from receiving yours. Now we all know that's not allowing us to be happy. One of the things that concerns me, is that some people, if they feel happiness coming on, they try to stop feeling it because they figure that once they are feeling happy something is going to be wrong.

Now come let's cut all that craziness out. It's all about happiness remember, we have one life to live and our one life by right is not supposed to be interrupted by no one, but if we do allow people close to us we shouldn't allow them to touch us, close is as far as it gets.

I wrote this inspirational, realistic book because of the necessity of reality, and even though I have all these experiences I still have a far way to go because I still get surprises. Remember we all know that we have to expect good and bad in life, but sometimes when things happen, we don't know whether they are good or bad for us. We need to come up with some different words for things that are happening these days. Confusion is all over the atmosphere these days, so when things happen or a person tells you what you want to hear, be careful. Not every thing that glitters is gold.

Be careful of deception because people are getting very deceiving these days. I know whatever is happening now, most of them are from the beginning of time, but they were wrong from the beginning, so nothing is wrong if we try to stop doing or indulging in what is wrong. We need to first make the changes in ourselves and if we can accept that the bad things are getting worse and try to correct what we can, then we will and can make a difference; so that our young generations can come up in a better world. Live like you have a responsibility or purpose, because you have one.

After my bad experiences in the Cayman Islands and I had returned home, I never thought that I could appreciate home that much. My love and appreciation for my home land Jamaica and my bed made me realize that the mistakes that I made that brought on those bad experiences were things I wanted no one else to experience.

A lot of us can relate to different experiences about trying to let a person know right from wrong, even trying to not let them make the mistakes you made or even what we have heard or seen, and by doing that, which is a good deed; we get in trouble with whosoever we are trying to help. Sometimes we even lose friendship, children going astray just by you trying to give them good advice.

Now these are some of the main things that causes people not to be happy. When we can get used to not being progressive or just simply finding a way out, it's hard or impossible to be happy when we are loving or caring for some one and trying to stop them from being unhappy and not to be asking the question why me in a negative way because of the things that they do or decisions they made and before you know it, it's like the worst thing we have ever done. Let's not forget we need each other so if we're given advice or instruction don't just push them off, but instead use what could be beneficial to you.

When we love, care, or want the best for someone, we have a responsibility to continue trying to coach them in the right direction and we can help to break the cycle of unhappiness. All we have to do is to do what we can and God will do the rest. We can love and care for some people, but after we keep trying to give them good directions, we have to allow them to live and decide if they want to take good counsel or they want to have their own experiences.

If we happen to encounter with people like those whether they are parents, children, or friends, we have no choice but to put them in the hands of the Almighty, because through him we find all the possibilities and what we can't do, all we have to do is ask him to do them for us.

Did you know that we are supposed to pray our lives through whatever it is we are going through or need? Not to mention our children because that's a must and if you don't have children, you still have a responsibility to pray for others. Now I'm not worried about a person that has a problem with us praying because we will pray for them so that they will start praying too.

Some things that we go through, only prayer can take us through. Now I strongly believe in prayer because with all the experiences, advice from other people or ourselves we still need God's covering because if we should know the amount of bad things and situations that he takes from us we would be amazed; we can't shut God out of our lives.

I know that a lot of people have a problem when we talk about God, because they don't like anything that would even make things right for them because their thing is just straight negativity. When you meet people like that just pray for them, but that's about it. We are working our way to happiness so there is no way we are going to see things or people that is bad for us and get involved.

Please let's start using what God gave us to guide us,

which is wisdom, let's not be anyone's fool. I'm really into helping people that really need a happy life, not for people who are into opposing every positive thing whether it's seen or personal experience. I don't understand why people would find it easier to gravitate to negative things. I understand they are easier to deal with but we have a life and not to mention some of us create lives and we are talking about beautiful children. Why choose the route that's not going to give you and your family real happiness not for a while or temporary?

I met a man, not a gentleman, however we greeted each other and it doesn't normally take me long to get down into some thanks giving conversation. When I started talking about the goodness of God and how blessed I am, he said, "My friend I don't know about that." Now I'm wondering what did I get myself into, because this man didn't believe the fact that he even had breath to talk to me; that's God's gift right there.

Now some of what he was saying I would not even put on paper because the thought of what he was saying scared me based on the honor I have for God. I realized that he needed a serious intervention from God because that one was too big for me to turn around. Now a person like that man, all we can do is really pray for them and God will do the work or he will determine where they are going because some people, "<u>dem write aff like ole vehicle</u>".

We don't need to know some people and the fact that

some people are really bad news, it takes God to direct us away from the ones that are really bad because they don't want what we want, which is happiness. They know that for whatever reason that they will never be happy.

Now this book is simple and straight forward. We have to start figuring different ways out in life. These days we are reading materials that's really not helping us with our lives so we have constant issues because some of what we read, if we really apply it to our lives, it can work against us because that's not our life or it wasn't meant for us. Don't forget my fantasies, all of that was imagination.

I can tell people, if you want to find time for recreation and break from the pressure of life with whatever situation, you need to take the time to pay special attention to the issues that are stopping or blocking your happiness, because we don't know when our lives will end.

"Every day we need to make the best of life, life is sweet. So are you ready to start finding ways and making changes? Because we can't afford to live selfishly and not think about who is behind or beside us, sometimes they are our moms, dads, sisters, brothers, partners, friends, children and or grandchildren, and the thing about all these bad situations is

that we can do something about some of them to make things better.

"There are three things that can cause us to go through some bad situations and they are whenever we are going to get a break through we don't display patience to see things manifest itself; two, when we allow things to happen to us; three, when we cause things to happen regardless of the fact that we knew the consequences. I hope you understand that whatever we 'sow' that is what we will reap."

Now a person would say I have been doing well all my life and all I'm getting is bad. No! That's not the case. You will reap good, it's just bad weeds that's coming up in your field, which is your life, and we simply have to deal with them. Bad things are a part of life but focus on what's good and the good seeds that you sow continue sowing because you will reap. It's just the bad situations trying to cover your good rewards.

There was a point in my life that I had to wonder if I could ever be happy again because every time things looked as if they were going to get better, just as they got close to the point where I would say thank you God because I'm seeing the possibilities, things would just tear down and that had me puzzled for a while. After wondering and praying for answers that I could make changes where necessary, I then came to the realization where I'm giving thanks for what I'm not receiving. Well there is so much to give thanks to God for that the thanks will fit somewhere.

"How can you give thanks if you didn't receive what you are giving thanks for? It's the norm for us to give thanks when we receive, but that wasn't my problem. My problem was that I leaned on my own understanding and saw things my way and not the Lord's. So because my understanding is limited, I desire things and venture in business that the Lord didn't approved of. Now if you ask me how would I know if and when the Lord approves, then I'm telling you that the things that I ventured in and even though it was a struggle, it still worked out, then that's all him. Now remember our timing is different from the Lord's so if he approves of what you started then he will allow you to pull through. Everyone would have to experience it for themselves, because he deals with each and every one of us in his own way and we all are dealt with differently."

Now for me he loves me so much that whatever I want that he has not approved of, then he makes it almost impossible; the little bit of possibility is the enemy. Try to allow what God doesn't approve of. Now where does that leave me? I have no choice but to start interceding.

"Sometimes things seem as if they cannot come together but ask in prayer and we have to have God on our side." Know the difference between God's love and the enemy's wide open opportunities to achieve what will tear you down whether it's financially, mentally, physically, and he always works hard on the spiritual side.

God operates like a loving mother or father that loves us so much that the things we want most of them they don't give them to us. They supply our needs, that's what they're catering for, but, didn't that make us mad when we were in our parent's care or still in their care? All because we didn't get what we wanted. Well it's the same thing with God. He will supply our needs, not the things that we want.

When we don't seek God's directions in our lives even from youth we choose career paths that were not for us. Our choices are often influenced by family and peers. Who told us that was going to work for us? Even though they work for other people and there may be a good financial gain it may not work for us. You may get to a point where you feel like everything is working the way you expected, but you are unhappy.

There is no way we should subject ourselves to the things that's interfering with our happiness. Our aim is to pluck them out and start creating the right approach to our real happiness and that's by getting to know what a mighty God we serve or some people should serve. Our biggest problem is no problem for him, just ask him for directions.

"When we do what's right we will be directed to the right job because sometimes we took some jobs based upon an opportunity to be in a certain position, and even though it's a job we got ourselves in other commitments within the job. Now if you really think about it, you knew that there were risks of being in trouble but you committed.

"I wonder how much some people really like or love themselves, because it's okay to cause ourselves harm, but it's not okay for another person to do it? I would say if you did that to yourself, what do you expect from other people? We should treat ourselves the way we want to be treated. How are we going to expect people to treat us with love and respect and we don't treat ourselves with love and respect?"

The value we place on our lives makes it hard for a person to value you less or more because they can disrespect you at any time because we can't control people and their behavior. That shouldn't devalue your standards; for example, when a man sees a female on the street and he knows that's a woman that he can look at, he going to route his approach correctly. His approach is based upon what he saw, whether he saw just a female or woman displaying lady like fashion.

Men in general tend to have respect for females, but it depends on the way a female adorns herself and operates. People incline to use a frown as a way of keeping people off but that will keep off some people that could enhance your life and attract the bad ones because it is most likely that people who wear a frown are not happy, so that's when another person that also wears a frown and that's most likely unhappiness. Now seeing you they tend to gravitate because they saw you in their group or figured that you would understand why they frown.

Remember you were just wearing a frown just to not sometimes communicate. When I personally see people on the road and I don't know them, and if I see them wearing a frown, I really don't try to say hi and the reason for that is because we are living in a troubled world and only God's directions can keep us away from making some simple mistakes that can turn into some big things.

"If we happen to see someone with a frown they may be on the brink and just a simple hello can throw them over the edge and I don't think you or I would want to be involved in any way. If we happen to see a smile it brings a sense of comfort and it's not easy to pass and don't say hello. A smile lifts your life up off the ground where a lot of us keep ours to collect dust. Let's shake ourselves off and smile for a while and give our face a rest, and we will start to attract happy people even though we may not be happy, that doesn't stop you from at least wearing one.

"I remember I saw a young lady and she had a serious frown, but something told me, well based upon the result it was God telling me to approach her with a smile, so I did and she asked me why am I smiling because she is not. So I said, "Where is mine?" She was wondering what I was talking about. So I said, "Give me back what I gave you", and she was like, "You didn't give me anything", then I said, "What about my pleasant smile", and I got her to start laughing and that caused

me to laugh because that created a different atmosphere."

I knew it was because God wanted me to make her day and at the end of the conversation, she said that the reason why she didn't smile was because she didn't have anything to smile about, but after talking to me she had at least five reasons and the first and fore most was life itself.

We already know that life is not the easiest thing to get together and the reason is because it's the most priceless thing and we can't put it away, we have to work with it every day. When something is priceless we can't leave it any where or give it away. Let's not use a frown to protect ourselves or when you have a problem because most times you can't protect your physical being and most times we have to leave it to God.

The best earthly protection is trying to wear a smile; that's the protection that we need on earth because when people see that smile it makes it harder for them to try to hurt you in any way, because in a spiritual way that's a sign of thanks giving. I know the things that we have to go through at our jobs, home, and with people in general. It's not easy to smile but a frown won't help.

All that does is show signs of depression and that's your weak moments, so instead people help you out of what you're going through, that's the time that they choose to dictate to you and just want to know your business because they saw a perfect opportunity. Remember not everyone wants to know you are going through bad situations, but the one that cares or can help, the fact that you put on that frown really scares them from even offering help.

Everyone should have pride but we need to be careful of pride because the pride that you need to have is the one that helps you. Sometimes we could or would get help with whatever we want or planning to pursue, but the fact that we act like we don't want or need help, then that automatically throw everything off.

Now why would a person help us when we are acting like we are okay or even in a better position than who is able to help? I can understand that it's not cool or good to show to the world that things are not good or you have a situation, but remember that the Bible said that we should ask and it shall be given. So when you are in need, just do not ask who you know will not give or who will criticize.

Now on the flip side, you don't want to ask some people for favors because that's the first opportunity to get at you about what they wanted to get at you with. They're people that wanted to curse or we would say cuss you out, and the fact that you ask for help or favor you could literally see and hear them warming up by coming off with sarcasm, asking questions and saying things that are hitting you in a way that you want to say forget it.

Well I guess when we remember that we really need that favor we would just back down. That's why it's good to make the right move, to listen, or cling to constructive counsel because that will help us to eliminate some of these favors. We are definitely not happy when someone embarrasses us just because we ask for help, so what do we do?

"Pride: you have to know when to display it. Live your life in a way that you have options, even in terms of people so you can ask the right persons for favors. A lot of time we know that the person we are planning on asking they are really not nice, but they are the only ones we either associate with or know. We don't want to be asking the questions "Why me & Where is my Happiness?", we only want to ask why me in a positive way and thanking God for happiness, because we are trying to live a life that could create a stunning, successful and endless happiness. As a writer I have a passion for people and nothing makes me feel better than when I see people trying to make positive moves."

Just to eliminate the stress of the world. It's so hard to know that this world is so perfectly created and we as a people who are God's most intelligent creatures, creating the stress on this land. Why are some people not living up to God's words such as we are our brother's keeper, and love thy neighbor as thy self? So if one should ask for help we all know it's not right to act or treat another person in a disrespectful manner or not displaying any compassion.

What about loving your neighbor as thy self? If you love you, you should love me, and there is nothing good you wouldn't do for your self, so you know that you should do it for me. Now I know that I am touching some delicate and controversial topics, but we all need real happiness.

I'm not trying to go around the route to create real happiness, which simply means that if you're trying to make me unhappy or you know that you could have made me happy by giving or even granting me a favor and didn't, that means you weren't my keeper and never loved me as a brother, now you're just creating the opposite of happiness. Well for those who don't know the opposite of happiness, it is sadness.

> *"Just imagine you are successful so things should be going good, but for some strange reason in other parts in your life you are having aches, sadness, disappointments, and if you should stop and look back in your*

life, you could very well find the answer to all those questions.

"Let's stop asking the question Why me? and Where is my happiness?, when we already know that if we did things in our lifetime good or bad they come right back at us (well for those who didn't know by now you should). I can understand that people do create a lot of things on themselves and block opportunities and joy, but we have a responsibility to change all that in us and if possible, help someone with a little guidance. Remember we are our brother's keeper; let's start living according to God's ordinance."

Don't allow ego to get in your way of progress or possible success or the most powerful thing in this world, and that's love. **Let's build love, not break down love** and also know when and who to love. You are the best and if nobody sees that, you already knew that. Be all that you can be, **live up, live big and surround your life with positive energy.** You can be who you want to be, only if you try, and with God's help nothing is impossible because greatness and peace belongs to you.

"This book is not intent on separating

things or people but most definitely bad habits, manipulation, and the stresses of poverty. You have one life to live and you don't know the length, so it's time to live it to its fullness and try to enjoy the rest of what you have. Remember life is priceless and it's not easy to see how some people live their's carelessly. Make yourself, family and friends proud. Focus on what's good and you will be on your way to a successful life.

Cling to constructive counsel, put on the armor of determination, because your intention is for a great, progressive and successful life. Then be prepared to be asked the question, "is that you?" It would be your pleasure to give them a big smile and say **yes it is me**. God has your back and you are on your way to a better life so please do not forget your reserved strength.

Never forget you will be tested.

I hope to publish other books to help you on **Life's journey**, it's time for reality, one love.

Peace